To God be the Glory!

Ron Schreuder

BROKEN
BUT NOT ABANDONED

*A Veteran's Journey
to Healing and Hope*

RONALD L. SCHWERMAN

with DAVID AEILTS

THE WORDSMITH

Bloomington, Minnesota

Cover and Interior Design: AuthorSupport.com

Edit by Grace Smith

Printed in the United States of America.

ISBN 978-0-9887356-0-6

Library of Congress Catalog Number 2012955358

Published by   The Wordsmith
                      5113 West 98th St. #138
                      Bloomington, Minnesota 55437
                      Phone: 612-240-9641
                      daeilts@comcast.net
                      www.wordschangedeverything.com

CONTENTS

PREFACE

Forty-five years ago, I lost two arms and a leg in a rocket attack. The intervening years have been a struggle, as you will read in these pages. But today I stand before you an intact human being. No, I did not grow new limbs; rather, I am complete inside and full of hope.

I wrote this book to let both veterans and civilians know there is life after the most traumatic of circumstances. Wounds may show outside or hide inside—usually both. Most injuries involve the spiritual aspect of our lives and can drive us to seek remedy in the wrong places.

My life is evidence of God's ability to heal and redirect the most damaged individual. My desire is that this book will help many find physical, psychological and spiritual wholeness. This is my story.

Yours truly,
Ron Schwerman

ACKNOWLEDGEMENTS

Thanks to all who have encouraged me on this journey. Special thanks to: **My wife Eydie**: Because you would not quit, you have opened doors I thought were closed forever. I treasure your love. **My parents Lawrence and Evelyn Schwerman**: You laid a foundation of faith. **My brother Leroy Knudson**: You gave me adult guidance when I needed it and introduced me back into faith. **Dr. Ernie Boswell**: You made valuable contributions to my story and the stories of many others. Thanks for your dedication to all of America's veterans. **Pastor Norman Schramm**: You answered my urgent call for help. **Jon Knutson**: You put an end to my pity party and were instrumental in saving my life. **Dr. Clayton Bawden**: I cherished your friendship, and your knowledge of PTSD was invaluable. **Barb Frank**: I am grateful for your friendship and support over the years and for your insights into this book. **Dave Aeilts**: You believed I had a story to tell and helped me shape the words.

Most importantly, I want to thank **my God and Savior Jesus Christ** who never gave up on me. You continue to love me unconditionally and inspire me daily.

DEDICATION

*"In every victory, let it be said of me: my source of
strength, my source of hope is Christ alone."*
—Brian Littrel, *In Christ Alone*,
Reunion Records, 2005.

CHAPTER 1

The Explosion

Da Nang Air Base
South Vietnam

0300 hours, 27 February 1967

The sound and smell of hot water trickling through a basket of ground roasted beans filled the one-room shack we called our office. It was time for a break, a cup of coffee, and a few cigarettes with the AGE night crew[1] at the south maintenance sub pool on Da Nang Air Base, Vietnam. The distant whine of an engine grew louder and nearer, followed by the squealing of brakes. "You guys got any coffee in there?" shouted Captain Anderson, as he pulled his jeep along the east wall of the screened-in office. The captain, our shop's administrative officer, was pulling extra duty as

---

1   **AGE** – the Aerospace Ground Equipment team, part of the 366th Field Maintenance Squadron (FMS) at Da Nang Air Base.

Officer of the Day in the early morning hours at what had become the world's second busiest airport.

South Vietnam made its first air strikes on the North from this base just eighty-five miles from the Demilitarized Zone.[2] As the war escalated, United States Air Force and Marine personnel and equipment swelled the air base beyond capacity. In the late '60s, the number of military and civilian aircraft taking off and landing exceeded 55,000 monthly—even more if you counted helicopters.[3]

The men of the south maintenance sub pool maintained and performed small repairs on ground power equipment like compressors and generators used to start hundreds of Air Force jets and propeller-driven aircraft taking off from the base each day.

We had constructed this maintenance shop at one end of Da Nang's twin 10,000-foot runways just a few months earlier, behind a U-shaped concrete revetment designed to shelter parked aircraft from attack. The sub pool's lean-to roof sloped about twenty feet out from the concrete wall and about fifty feet along it. We drove four-by-four studs into the ground every ten feet to support the roof. It was all we needed for shelter from the heavy monsoon rains while working on the equipment. Our small, makeshift office stood at one end of the lean-to.

Hanging from the ceiling of that office, a bare bulb illuminated the sparse furnishings—one desk, a couple of chairs, an old blue

---

2   **Demilitarized Zone** – A supposedly combat free zone between North and South Vietnam.

3   http://en.wikipedia.org/wiki/Da Nang Air Base

bus seat we had scavenged from the bone yard, and a coffee maker purchased at the Marine PX, along with cups and sugar and cream.[4] A radio on the desk blared big band and classical music bookended by the enticing voice of Hanoi Hanna as she tried to discourage or frighten our troops with stories of their wives' unfaithfulness and the heroic achievements of the enemy. We laughed at most of what she said, but occasionally she succeeded at making us feel a bit homesick.

On dark, moonless mornings like this one, with our perimeter lighting extending no more than 100 feet to the east, the warm glow and smell of coffee emanating from the sub pool office was inviting. At 0300 hours, I took my place on the bus seat, the most comfortable spot in the office. Staff Sergeant James Beal sat behind the desk and greeted Captain Anderson as he opened the screen door.

"Good Morning, Sir," said Sergeant Beal. I nodded as the brass walked in and grabbed a cup. I was only an Airman First Class (A1C) and my first thought was to let Captain Anderson have my seat. My next thought was, *"To hell with that!"* After all, I was wearing my "short-timer's ribbon" which I'd taken from an empty VO whiskey bottle.[5] Less than two weeks from today, I'd be leaving

---

4 **Bone yard** – A junk yard at the Da Nang Air Base containing parts of airplanes and other vehicles that had crashed or had been discarded for other reasons.

5 **Short-timer** – Military personnel who had almost completed their year-long deployment to Vietnam were known as short-timers. Being "short" was a source of pride to these men and women who displayed their most-favored status by pinning a ribbon from a VO whiskey or bourbon bottle to their shirts. Everyone knew these ribbon-bearers were going home soon.

Vietnam for the States and my discharge from the Air Force. At this point, I felt no compulsion to bow to authority.

In my pockets that morning, I carried my discharge orders and a small hand-made calendar on which I checked off the days until 10 March when A1C Ron Schwerman (that's me) would leave this hot, muggy land colored in drab olives and grays and smelling of blood.

It seemed strange now that I was almost on my way home, but for the past twelve months I'd had a sixth sense that I would be wounded, even though the air base was a relatively safe place. I was sure I wouldn't be killed, but maybe I'd get hit with shrapnel from small mortars the Viet Cong (VC) had begun to lob at the base. Then again, maybe this sixth sense was just some crazy idea my mind conjured up to deal with the stress of war and being away from home.

This close to my discharge, all I could think of was seeing my wife and two daughters back in Minnesota. Oh how I longed to be home! I was even wearing my wedding ring that morning, despite regulations prohibiting jewelry as a hazard on the job.

My stomach turned when I thought of the long plane ride back to the states. I never had gotten used to flying and often wondered why I ever joined the Air Force. When I was a child, I loved to watch airplanes flying overhead; but as an adult, I certainly didn't enjoy being in them. *"It will all be over in a few days,"* I thought, consoling myself. *"I'll never have to fly again."* Beyond my fear of flying, I felt like a lot of people in their twenties—in control of my future. I was leaving Vietnam safely and in one piece.

Whether based in reality or not, my optimism contrasted with the pessimism of another A1C, a friend of mine named Bob Jones. Through the screened-in walls of the office that morning, I could see Jones climbing out of his tractor after delivering a generator to an aircraft on the flight line. He moved slowly, like he did every morning in Vietnam, as if he only had one gear. Jones told me his parents had split when he was young, and I guess he never got over it. *"Maybe he'll straighten out when he gets back to the States,"* I thought. *"You just can't go through life as bitter and depressed as he is and get along with people."*

0310 HOURS, 27 FEBRUARY 1967

Boom! An extremely loud explosion shook the office, like some fireworks you hear on the Fourth of July when you get too close. The sound came from the other side of the revetment. *"Maybe the VC are trying to hit the birds inside,"* I thought, picturing the F-4C phantom jets that had been parked behind the concrete wall. Too bad! They left earlier to fly cover for a bombing mission up north.

BLAM! Another even louder blast shook the building in the direction of the electronics shop. Now I was on my feet. "They're hitting all over the place," said Sergeant Beal, "and they're awful damn big!" Looking for cover, I realized someone else—probably Beal—was already under the desk. Thinking I could make it 100 feet to the bunker, I headed out of the office.

With my arms straight in front of me, I was just pushing open the screen door when I noticed Jones outside and to my right. Then it hit. WHAM!

It seemed like I flew through the air and hit a wall, but I couldn't remember dropping to the ground. *"I must have fallen and my lights went out,"* were my next thoughts. *"We took a pretty good hit. That blast must have been close."*

Feeling no pain, I wanted to get up and start running, but I couldn't move or even feel my arms and legs. *"What the hell is the matter with me?"* I wondered. *"Why can't I get up?"* I lay on my side, watching little pieces of white hot metal trailing streams of smoke falling all around me. Everything was happening in slow motion. Then it dawned on me, *"I'm hit—BAD! Oh God, PLEASE help me!"* A wave of panic swept over me. I'd never felt fear like I felt at that moment—fear of dying. I wanted to vomit.

I have no idea how long I lay there, but all of a sudden I became aware of someone touching me. *"It's going to be okay now,"* I thought. *"They know I'm alive."* That's when I heard a Navy corpsman say, "This son-of-a-bitch is dead." Horrified at his words, I screamed with all my might: *"I'M NOT DEAD! I'M ALIVE!"* But the corpsman didn't seem to hear. I felt him wrapping me in a red-colored blanket—or was that my blood?

The corpsman started to throw me in a pile with three other bodies but decided instead to throw me into a truck. I flew through the air, and as my body hit the floor, I heard a wounded soldier in that truck exclaim, "Oh, my God!" I couldn't understand why the corpsman was handling me so roughly. Then he told someone in the truck not to put me on a stretcher. "Just leave him on the floor," he said. "The son-of-a-bitch is dead, and I need the stretchers for the wounded." At that, I lost consciousness.

"The cords of death entangled me; the torrents of destruction overwhelmed me. The cords of the grave coiled around me, the snares of death confronted me. In my distress, I called out to the Lord; I cried to my God for help."—Psalm 18: 4-6a (NIV)

FIRST ROCKETS OF THE WAR

The U.S. observed a truce during Tet, the lunar New Year, a traditional Vietnamese holiday. The truce lasted from 9 February through 12 February 1967. On 13 February President Lyndon B. Johnson announced that peace efforts had failed and the U.S. would resume full-scale bombing of North Vietnam. On 22 February U.S. and South Vietnamese forces launched the largest military offensive of the war.[6] Five days into that offensive, North Vietnamese and Viet Cong forces staged the attack on Da Nang Air Base that injured Ron Schwerman and killed A1C Robert H. Jones, 20, Arlington, Virginia. Subsequent attacks earned the base the nickname "Rocket City."

The 27 February attack was the first to employ 140 mm unguided rockets. All previous attacks involved mortars. The Russian-made 140 mm rocket was four feet long and contained about ten pounds of high explosives. Its fuse fired on impact.[7] In total, the enemy launched more than fifty rockets during that pre-dawn attack, killing eleven and wounding 124.[8]

---

6   Vietnam War (1965-1968): Timeline, Facts, and Resources, Research by F.Rosseti, http://www.thefreeresource.com/vietnam-war-1965-1968-timeline-facts-and-resources

7   EOD in Vietnam 1966-1967, Photo Album, http://www.zianet.com/tmorris/vnalbum.htm (accessed April 29, 2011)

8   A high number of casualties were Vietnamese civilians living in a village just east of Da Nang Air Base. http://www.366fightergroupassoc.org/Attacks.htm (accessed April 29, 2011)

CHAPTER 2

Growing Up in Minneapolis

St. Mary's Hospital
Minneapolis, Minnesota

February 22, 1944

A common notion about what happens when you are mortally wounded is that your entire life flashes before your eyes. That was not my experience; however, it might be helpful to rewind the tape of time and describe a little of what I might have seen, had that notion been true for me.

Twenty-three years and five days before that early morning rocket attack, I was born at St. Mary's Hospital in Minneapolis. I spent my preschool years in a working class neighborhood known as Cedar-Riverside, east of downtown. Our house, at

617 South Sixteenth Avenue, was half-a-block from the railroad tracks. As kids, we'd boost each other onto passing trains and ride a few blocks downtown. I also remember pulling my wagon down to a siding where workers unloaded freight cars. They'd toss me broken melons and other unsalable but fresh produce, and I'd bring those treasures back home to my mother, Evelyn Mary (Leslie) Schwerman.

My father, Lawrence Carl Schwerman, worked for the Milwaukee Railroad before and after serving with the Army Air Corps in the South Pacific during World War II.

As a railroad tower man, Dad operated a system of signals warning the public of approaching trains.[1] When I was older, my dad let me visit his tower, turn on the semaphore lights, and ring the bells as the trains came through. Once he told me of a man hard of hearing who was trapped between two trains. The man got confused and fell under the heavy wheels to his demise.

My immediate family consisted of my mother, my father, a brother named LeRoy B. Knutson, who was fifteen years older than me, and a younger sister, Carol Jean. LeRoy was born to my mother in 1929 through a previous marriage. Her first husband, Roy Knutson, had died, and in 1942, she married my father. My sister Carol Jean, born in 1946, contracted spinal meningitis as an infant, leaving her totally deaf.

---

1   Lawrence Schwerman was the longest working and last remaining tower man in the Minneapolis-St. Paul area before the railroad installed automatic signals and phased out towers.

Many of my early childhood memories revolve around Cedar Avenue, a thoroughfare less than two blocks from our house. I attended kindergarten at Clay School on Riverside Avenue, just off Cedar. My kindergarten teacher supplied one of my first recollections of discipline. We were lying on our mats during nap time, but I wouldn't quiet down. Finally, my teacher had enough of my babbling and taped my mouth shut.

As a young child, I was extremely gullible. Walking home from kindergarten one day, an older boy convinced me the drug store at Sixth and Cedar was running a promotion. "If you take anything without them seeing," he told me, "you can have it for free." Believing him, I promptly took two toy knives with blades that recessed into the handle when you stabbed someone. I gave one knife to the older boy and took one home. Later that day, my mother saw the knife. Realizing I had not paid for it, she and my Dad marched me down to the drug store and made me give it back. I remember the druggist saying, "Oh, let him have it." "No, he can't," said my mother, giving me an early lesson in honesty.

Other memories center on the Cedar Theater just a short walk from our home, where I could spend an afternoon at the movies for a quarter. Often, I'd find myself looking back at the projector and wondering how it worked. Once, I went back to my house and upstairs to my room where I wound up a toy train. I let the train run while I shined a flashlight on it, trying to project a picture on the wall. I couldn't figure out why it wouldn't work. Another time, I saw a rocking horse in the theater window. Movie patrons could throw their tickets in a drawing for that horse. I remember wanting it so badly, but of course I didn't win it. Still another time, Mom gave me a quarter for the movies and promptly forgot I had gone to the theater. After the show, I walked home to learn that my frantic mother had all the neighbors out looking for me.

In those days after WWII, there were a lot of airplanes flying over the Cedar-Riverside neighborhood. It seemed like the sky was full of them, and occasionally they dropped advertising leaflets. I was excited about those flying machines, so I asked my dad to build me one with a propeller that would actually spin. In my young mind, I thought that plane would fly.

My elementary years

When I was six years old, my mom and dad bought a four-plex building in the Elliot Park neighborhood, southeast of downtown Minneapolis. We moved into the bottom, left-hand apartment at 611 East Sixteenth Street and rented out the other three. This would be my home until I joined the military.

Located between Portland and Chicago Avenues, ours was a nice neighborhood with lots of trees and well-kept houses. Founded by Swedish immigrants in the 1850s, many residents of this prestigious area of the city were well-off in the early 1900s. By the time we moved there in September 1950, the neighborhood was more diverse and mostly blue collar—including us. I started first grade at Madison Elementary School just across Portland Avenue.

In this neighborhood, I formed the friendships of my youth. I experienced the community's diversity and similarities, like its pervasive battle with alcohol. My friend Dennis' mother was for all practical purposes a single parent, as Dennis' dad was a drunk. My friend Jim's dad belonged to a northern Minnesota Indian tribe. He, too, wrestled with alcohol. The parents of my best friend Neil were also alcoholics and collected welfare for years while his dad battled throat cancer. Assorted in their ethnic origins, our families were also diverse in their religious beliefs. Jim was a Catholic, as was Neil. Another friend named Jim was a Protestant like me.

Of German ancestry, my dad was a devout Christian and knew the Bible fairly well. His father (my grandfather) was a Lutheran pastor and very strict. He was also a teacher, and the Bible was a pretty big deal in their family. The daughter of an Englishman, Ma grew up Catholic and became a Lutheran when she married Dad. He would faithfully take my sister Carol and me to Sunday school when we were children. I'm certain that had an effect on my view of the world as I was growing up.

One scene that looms large in my memory is of Dad at the kitchen table and Ma in the living room watching TV. Dad was drinking a beer and working a crossword puzzle. Before bed, I'd often come in and sit on a stool and shoot the breeze with Dad. This particular evening, we were talking about people who don't believe in Jesus Christ. He told me, "Those people are going to hell." For some reason, his statement scared me to death. I remember going to bed that night and almost being in tears thinking about whether I would go to hell.

We had some dirty laundry, like any family. My mother and father fought a lot, and some of those fights were pretty bad. Ma could get really mad and lose control. Dad could also get very mad when pushed to the limit, but was generally more easygoing.

One time they had a disagreement over drinking beer. Dad would buy a case of Kingsbury, the cheapest beer you could buy. I don't know what the fight was about, but Ma dumped all his beer down the drain. She said she wasn't having any more beer in the house. At that point, Dad began going down to the Fourth Avenue bars to have his beer, until Ma finally said he could have it at home again.

I don't remember my dad ever hitting my mom, though at times he may have wanted to. He certainly did get mad enough. One time, he went to bed early because he had to get up early for work. Apparently he and Ma had had a fight, and she was on the phone right outside their bedroom door, telling her mother how big an ass he was. All of a sudden, Dad came out of the bedroom, grabbed the phone, ripped it out of the wall, set it down, and quietly went back to bed.

My parents were loving, too. At least in my earlier years, they would kiss around us, and to their credit they stayed together.

At the time we moved to the Elliot Park neighborhood, my brother Leroy was married and living just off Franklin Avenue. He served in the Marine Reserve and the U.S. Marine Corps called him to active duty during the Korean Conflict. Before leaving, LeRoy moved his wife LaVonne and their children to an apartment at Sixteenth Street and Chicago Avenue, just a couple blocks away from us, where they lived while he was in Korea.

LeRoy was involved in some heavy fighting at the Battle of Chosen Reservoir. His entire division was over-run by the Chinese, and almost everyone was killed. LeRoy was hit by small mortar fire and went down. Lying on the ground for two to three days with Chinese soldiers jumping over his body, LeRoy came close to dying before being rescued and flown out to Japan to save his feet from frostbite. My brother told me that only six truckloads of U.S. Marines from his division made it out of Korea alive.

Right around Christmas 1950, as I recall, we heard a knock at the door and there stood LeRoy. I don't think I understood at that time how much danger he had been in, but I do remember being kind of a big shot in the neighborhood because my brother served in the Marine Corps. Among my friends at that time, we had the "my brother can beat your brother up" mindset, and it was understood that my brother LeRoy could take them all.

With elementary school came the opportunity for my friends and me to broaden our interests. I was pretty heavy into stamp and coin collecting and had friends that collected. I also liked art, and a friend of mine named Gerry was an unbelievable artist. He could draw like nobody else, and we built a lot of models out of balsa wood, but my models never turned out quite as good as his. I also had friends that I'd go with to the public library down on Hennepin Avenue, just to look at books.

In the early years, I was still a bit naive. One time, Ma gave me some money and asked me to run an errand at Manila's Grocery a few doors down from our apartment. When I entered the store, I met an older girl named Nancy, who I knew through her brother Johnny. Nancy convinced me that I could give her some of the change from my shopping trip and that I wouldn't be short. So I did, and headed for home with the wrong change. I had to explain, of course, and Ma was hoppin' mad. She made a beeline to Manila's Grocery to get the facts and then to the school where she confronted Nancy about the trouble she'd made for me.

As I grew older, however, I learned how to make my own trouble. Once, my friends and I wrote all over a neighbor's garage door with a compound left over from the dry cleaning process. It looked like mud and was hard to wash off. I ought to know. The neighbor told our parents, and they made us remove every word we'd written on that door. It took hours.

My best friend Neil and I tried smoking in a vacant apartment next door, and I got violently ill. Another time while I was delivering newspapers, I found a box of prophylactics on the corner of Sixteenth Street and Park Avenue. I inflated them like balloons and left them all along my paper route between Portland and Park, on Sixteenth and Seventeenth Streets.

TEENAGERS IN TROUBLE

As I entered my teen years, I dabbled in more serious delinquency. My friends and I started shoplifting from Kresge's and other downtown department stores. They caught us a couple of times, but just took our names and let us go. We'd also go out drinking. Although underage, we found plenty of older people willing to buy our alcohol. When sufficiently inebriated, we'd taunt the police into chasing us. Pursued late one night, we hid on the east side of Madison Elementary School, while a patrol car shined its spotlight back and forth across the school grounds, searching for us. On another occasion, an officer we had taunted actually caught and arrested us. He took us to jail, but Juvenile Court gave us a hand-slap and probation.

Somewhere along the line, my parents lost control of me. They had their hands full with my sister who was deaf and had to attend special schools. I don't blame them. They were good examples in my life. I remember Dad walking downtown to pay bills. On the way back, he found a wallet on the sidewalk at the corner of Seventeenth Street and Portland. The wallet contained a wad of money from a cashed payroll check. Dad knew the owner lived in the apartment building on that corner, and he returned the money to him. So I knew right from wrong, but I wasn't being disciplined. I was running wild with my friends.

The influence of organized religion was also waning. After grade school, I no longer attended Sunday school, and some of my friends had paper routes which gave them extra money to spend. That really appealed to me, so at eleven years old, I got my own paper route. Having to deliver the paper early on Sunday morning contributed to my not attending church at all.

My brother LeRoy could see what was happening to me. I admired LeRoy. He was very involved in the Lutheran church. He was also a coin and stamp collector. (Maybe that's why I took up those hobbies.) Like Dad, LeRoy worked for the Milwaukee Railroad. Later he switched to the Great Northern Railroad.

With fifteen years between us, LeRoy was more like a father to me than a brother. He and I would talk, usually when he was driving me home from babysitting his kids. Mostly, he would lecture me.

I give him and my mother credit for trying to get me back into church. They talked me into getting confirmed. I didn't understand exactly what confirmation was, just that it was something I was supposed to do. I had a poor understanding of what Christianity was all about and why my family went to church. It just wasn't important in my mind. I think I believed in God, but I was not living as a Christian.

The pastor who confirmed me, however, made a strong impression on me. I saw Martin H. Kretchmeyer, who was an Army chaplain as well as a pastor, as a devout Christian whom I trusted. Like my brother LeRoy, Martin was legit, and I had high respect for him.

While studying for my confirmation, I served as an acolyte in my church. As such, I was responsible for lighting candles and controlling the lighting in the sanctuary. I'd get to church early Sunday morning and don my gown. Then, I'd set the rheostat in the pastor's office, which controlled the lighting in the sanctuary. I remember being awfully nervous when I went up to light the candles. I'd just shake. I've always had a fear of being in front of people, and especially of speaking in public.

At one point, Pastor Kretchmeyer sat me down and asked me about becoming a minister. He said the church would help with my schooling. I used my fear of standing up and speaking in front of people as an excuse for not going into ministry. The truth was, I was unwilling to live a Christian lifestyle. In my middle teens, girls and drinking were becoming a much bigger factor in my life than religion. I was not about to give up these pleasures, even to impress a man I admired.

Then, at age fifteen, I bought a gun.

CHAPTER 3

Coming of Age Badly

Downtown Minneapolis

1959

I waited, along with my best friend Neil, outside the small gun shop at Fifteenth Street and Nicollet Avenue. Inside, my twenty-one-year-old girlfriend Cathy paid for two gas-operated pellet guns and some ammunition. I looked older than I was and probably lied to Cathy about my age the evening I met her in a neighborhood park, just to get in bed with her. But at fifteen, Neil and I were too young to buy guns. No problem. Cathy was more than willing to buy them for us, along with our beer and booze.

Later, she bought us nine-shot .22 caliber revolvers. They were small and fit easily in our pants pockets.

It was fun to practice firing at trees and tin cans, but our purpose was darker. Elliot Park was a tough neighborhood, even in the late

21

'50s, and we thought the guns would make us invincible. It never occurred to us that someone tougher might have a bigger gun and wouldn't hesitate to use it.

Besides, carrying a gun fit my dicey lifestyle.

It started with weekend drinking parties with classmates from Phillips Junior High in southeast Minneapolis. By my upper teens, I was on my way to becoming an alcoholic. I was handsome, too, and I didn't have a hard time getting girls, so sex became a big factor in my life.

People I respected did their best to correct me. On Sunday mornings, I delivered the *Minneapolis Tribune* newspaper in our neighborhood. My route manager was an Italian named Maroney. He called once when I was fighting with my mother. Over the phone, Maroney heard me screaming and swearing at her. Later, he took me aside and told me in no uncertain terms that I needed to change my behavior.

My brother LeRoy, who I greatly admired, tried his best to pull me away from the sex and booze. He brought me back to church, got me into confirmation classes, and helped me join a softball team sponsored by our church; but it was too late. I was already involved in those other things—and now, at fifteen, I was carrying a gun with little understanding of its appropriate use.

On one occasion, three tough guys knocked on the door of another girlfriend's apartment near Loring Park. I answered the door. "We want to see Sue," they declared. I stepped outside the door to challenge them: "Why do you want to see Sue?" No answer, but one of them pulled a knife, and I recognized the other as one of Sue's former boyfriends. "Okay," I said quickly and ducked back inside. Instead of telling Sue, I went straight to the bedroom closet and got my gun. Bursting from the apartment, I fired two shots into the ceiling of the hallway, which sent the tough guys running to the front and back stairs. For good measure, I fired two more shots toward the back stairwell and may have hit one of the guys. Neil, who was also there, spotted one of the guys sitting on the back steps, crying and holding his foot.

Before police could respond to the shots, we grabbed our gear and left the building. On the way out, we looked up and saw that another friend of mine, Jerry, had jumped out a bedroom window. He was hanging from a ledge. We all laughed and thought that was so funny. Truth was, we were all drunk, and everything we did seemed hilarious. It was a poor time to be waving a gun.

A POOR CHOICE OF FRIENDS

To make matters worse, at age sixteen I began hanging around with a guy twice my age, and according to rumor, he had shot a cop in Indiana. As it was later explained to me, Roger was driving a car loaded with stolen stuff and was pulled over by a highway patrolman. He grabbed the trooper's gun and killed him with it. Why he spent only seven years in an Indiana reformatory I don't know. But when he moved to Minnesota, he spent time in Stillwater where he was in charge of the prison newspaper.

I met Roger after he got out of prison, and I guess he appealed to me because he was older. He got us alcohol and loaned us his car to pick up girls and bring them into town for partying and sex at his apartment.

One night, Roger was driving Neil and me down the Midway neighborhood when, suddenly, we were surrounded by patrol cars. The cops took us to the St. Paul Police Department where they put Roger in jail and called our parents.

Dad refused to come and get me. "To hell with it," he said. "Let him do what he is going to do." I had gotten into a few fights with Dad that almost turned physical, and I had pulled a knife on him one time. He came at me with the intention of taking the knife away and cut his hand in the process. I think Dad was through taking my abuse.

Instead, my brother LeRoy drove my mother and Neil's mother over to St. Paul to pick us up.

I should have realized Roger was not the kind of guy to hang out with, but a few nights later I found myself alone in his apartment. He asked me to help him open a safe he had gotten out of a gas station, and naively I agreed. We drove to his parent's garage in south Minneapolis, where we spent two to three hours breaking into the safe with drills and saws. We removed some cash, checks, change, stamps and other things. After that, we hauled the safe down to Lake Street and crossed into St. Paul. Somewhere along River Road, we threw the safe into the Mississippi River. The fact that I didn't personally break into the gas station must have made it okay in my warped young mind to help my "friend" open the safe. Besides, Roger was my benefactor, the source of liquor and a flop-house for sex.

Then something happened to clarify my view of this older man. Roger let me have his car and his downstairs apartment at Fourth Avenue and Tenth Street for the weekend. It was wintertime, and he said he was taking a couple girls skiing. "We won't be back until Monday," he assured me. The apartment was well stocked with alcohol and food, and with the use of Roger's Pontiac, I could pick up a girlfriend, Gail, who lived in the suburbs. Driving out to her house, I drank a quart of beer. When I brought my girlfriend downtown to Roger's apartment, we ended up in bed and drank even more.

Gail left the next morning, and I honestly don't remember what I did for the rest of the weekend, but I was back in school by Monday when my friend Roger returned. Later that week Neil and I sat drinking coffee at a restaurant when detectives from the Minneapolis Police Department burst in. They let Neil go, but they put me in a squad car and took me downtown. After some initial questioning, a detective informed me, "We've got Roger upstairs in jail, and he is saying you used his car to commit several burglaries last weekend."

Come to find out, Roger had left the apartment with several ski masks he wore to burglarize gas stations. The cops had tracked him down, and now he was fingering me. At that point, I opened up and told them everything they wanted to know. Although I was underage, I told them I was down in Roger's apartment drinking with my girlfriend, Gail. That was my alibi. But I went even further. I told them about the night I helped Roger open the safe and where we dumped it.

The detective asked if I could identify a New York friend of Roger's who they suspected of helping him with the gas station burglaries. I told them I could, so they released me. The next day the detective got me out of school and took me down to the bus depot. He parked a block away and instructed me to "walk over to the depot, go upstairs, go into the bathroom and then come back and tell me if Roger's friend is in there. If he is, tell me what he's wearing."

I did as the detective asked. Sure enough, the man was in the depot. When I got back to the cop car, the detective advised me to go back to school. Not willing to walk that far, I refused. Instead, I said, "I want to see his face when you arrest him." So I sat in the front seat on the passenger side and watched as the detective came back with the suspect in handcuffs and stowed him safely in the back seat. When the guy I fingered saw me, he asked if they'd gotten me also. "No," I said foolishly. "I'm the one who turned you in." The detective drove this guy to jail and then drove me back to school.

Later, Roger told Neil that the New Yorker was out to kill me for fingering him. I remember walking down the stairs at the bus station and meeting the New Yorker walking up. "I got my .45 out in the trunk," he sneared. I decided to act tough. I pulled out my

.22 caliber and waved it at him. "You want to go? Let's go!" I boasted. The gun was loaded, but fortunately nothing ever came of the challenge. I wasn't as tough as the gun made me out to be.

MY RESPECTABLE DELINQUENCY ENDS

It might sound like I was a small time hood, but in fact I led a double life. On weekends I drank and slept around, but I always made it to school on Monday mornings and was a bit of a nerd, as opposed to my Baldy and Greaser friends. The Baldies wore Ghant shirts, tight high-wasted jeans and re-enforced wingtip shoes. They fought with their legs—kicking instead of punching. The Greasers wore their hair long and carried long metal combs with the back side filed into a blade with which they "slashed" their rivals. On the other hand, I got my hair cut regularly, wore work clothes from Kaplins Clothing down on Franklin and Seventeenth Avenue, and held a series of fairly good jobs. I was even planning to continue my study of electronics after high school. True, I could have done a whole lot better if I had put my nose to the grindstone, but I was too interested in girls and alcohol.

As for my gun, Ma found it in a drawer in my bedroom and said I couldn't get a car until I let her have the gun. So much for the tough guy—I gave the gun up immediately. She and Dad turned it over to my brother, LeRoy, who was a Reserve Minneapolis Police officer and knew what to do with it.

Though I'd never been sentenced to jail for my drinking and other misdemeanors, my lifestyle finally caught up with me in my senior year at Vocational High School, downtown Minneapolis. Neil and I got picked up again for underage drinking. Juvenile Court had already placed us on probation twice. This time the courts decided to send us to the Glen Lake Reform School, a twenty-one-day disciplinary program. They let us graduate from high school before going to Glen Lake, and even though I would turn eighteen before entering the program, they still dealt with me as a juvenile.

Glen Lake was operated like a boot camp. We marched in formation everywhere we went, and we were never alone, even going to the bathroom. For the brief term of the camp, we lost our privacy and freedom to move around as we pleased. The campers ranged from ten-year-olds to eighteen-year-olds and some were pretty tough. One kid at camp that summer had murdered his parents. Some campers, like Neil and me, were not so tough. We weren't capable of robbing a store or killing anybody.

I don't know how much good Glen Lake did me. I continued to drink, but I think it stuck in my head that going to jail or prison was not something I wanted to do. They were trying to teach me a lesson, and I got at least part of the lesson.

The thing I remember most clearly from Glen Lake was this one statement: "You are at the end of your joy ride as a teenager, Schwerman," said one counselor. "From now on, if you get caught, you'll be treated as an adult."

CHAPTER 4

Marriage to the Military

Downtown Minneapolis

Fall 1962

The September following my high school graduation, I went back to Vocational High School for post-grad courses in electronics. I loved electronics and wanted to work in that field or in the newly developing computer field.

One afternoon after classes, Neil and I stopped by Keller's Drug at the corner of Fourteenth Street and Chicago Avenue.[1] We sat at the counter and ordered Cokes. The waitress, Judie Duncan, greet-

---

1 Keller's Drug later became Griswold Drug.

ed me by name. When I asked her how she knew me, she said, "My sister Donna was in several of your classes at Philips Junior High."

I wouldn't say Judie flirted with me, but she was very nice and showed me more than normal interest. She was two years my junior, with a cute figure and nice legs. Come to find out, she was studying sewing and tailoring at Vocational High School.

Judie and I talked whenever I stopped at the drug store, and eventually I asked her to a homecoming football game. A woman named Betty, who worked as a cook at in the drug store, encouraged her to go. After our first date, Judie and I got pretty close. Soon we were going steady.

While the electronics I studied at Vocational High School interested me, I was sick of the traditional classroom and wanted a change. So I decided to quit school and join the military. I could have volunteered for the draft and been done in two years, but I wanted more training in electronics and the opportunity to travel. I decided to enlist.

Judie was not happy about my decision, but she realized that going into the service was a way to move forward. I could either go to college or be drafted, and as I mentioned, I was sick of the traditional classroom. There were no real jobs available until one of the two, military service or higher education, was accomplished. And I really wasn't thinking very far ahead.

At the time, Judie's brother Lee was leaving the U.S. Air Force. I talked to Lee by phone, and he told me about his branch of the service. Another friend, Tommy Johnson, was a Marine and encouraged me to enlist in his branch.

My decision concerning which branch of the service to join came down to who was out-to-lunch, literally.

On a late fall day in 1962, I headed for the Federal Building at 212 Third Avenue South, downtown Minneapolis. The U.S. Navy and the U.S. Air Force appeared to be my best options. I thought of the Marine Corps as a little more physical and competitive than I wanted.

It was just after noon, and as I recall, I went to the Navy recruiter's office first. The recruiter was out-to-lunch. I passed by the Marines office, and that recruiter was out-to-lunch, too. But the Air Force recruiter was in. After talking with him briefly, I spent the rest of the afternoon taking a test and headed home.

I passed the test, scoring high on electrical, mechanical and administrative questions. The Air Force notified me that they would accept me. Because of my previous run-ins with the law, however, they would need a waiver from the Minneapolis Police Department to make sure there were no outstanding warrants against me. For this reason, I had to wait several months to join. To this day I think they were holding on to me to fill their spring quota. No doubt many recruits want to get away during the cold Minnesota winters, but not a lot want to join in the spring. That may be why they made me wait.

Despite my Glen Lake warning and my new-found girl friend, my love affair with alcohol continued. Judie and I attended a New

Years Eve party with a number of friends who also hung out at Keller's Drug. As usual, I'd been drinking heavily and was about to start a fight with a guy I thought was coming on to Judie when someone picked me up from behind and tossed me onto the porch. My assailant was our host, a big man who was afraid my belligerence would get everyone in trouble.

It was very cold out, and I was sitting there nursing my wounds when Judie came out. "Let's leave," she suggested. We walked to my car parked in back and got in. All of a sudden a tough crowd of guys and girls looking for a fight surrounded our car. Most of the intruders attended Roosevelt High School and most of the kids I hung out with attended Central High School or Vocational High School.

This crowd was very hostile and ordered us out of the car. I started the car, rolled down the window, and told them we were leaving, so they let us go. Turning onto the street, I went about a quarter of a block and stopped. Instead of continuing to drive as Judie urged, I got out of the car, opened the trunk and pulled out the tire iron. "They came to kick our butts," I fumed. "I'm going back to kick theirs."

When I arrived back at the house, the intruders were gathered in the yard. I waved the tire iron and told them to "come and get it." There was one big problem. I was very drunk. Soon the tire iron was no longer in my hand, and I lay flat on the ground in the ice and snow. I'd been clobbered from behind and knocked half silly by a liquor bottle. (Someone later told me it was a girl who hit me, which added insult to injury.) While I was down, the intruders kicked and punched me. Then, as quickly as it started, it was over. The intruders left, and Judie, who fought with the girls and got her long gray coat all dirty, helped me back to our car.

I was a bloody mess, but despite the lump on my head, I insisted on driving. We went to my house first to clean up and then to Judie's home. I thought her parents would kill me when they found out I'd been in a fight. Instead, they invited me in for coffee and we talked. They genuinely liked me. Judie and I had become pretty close by that time, and they had accepted us as a couple despite my shortcomings.

BOUND FOR BOOT CAMP

Finally, I was ordered by the U.S. Air Force to report for duty on 17 April 1963 at the Federal Building. I had my physical and was sworn in right there along with other Air Force recruits. They loaded us into cabs with all of our paperwork for the ride to the airport. We boarded a commercial flight—an old DC3 that we later learned to call a *goony bird*—and began a slow, terrible flight to Texas.

It was the first time I had ever flown, and I was scared to death. After several bouts of nausea from turbulence, I remember asking the stewardess to bring something for my upset stomach. We flew non-stop to Dallas, then continued in the same plane to San Antonio, Texas where I would enter boot camp at Lackland Air Force Base.

We arrived at San Antonio International Airport at 0430 hours the following morning, and the Air Force loaded us onto buses for the cross-town trip to Lackland. At the air base, we thought we'd be able to get some sleep before they put us to work. That was not the case. Sergeant White, one of our tactical instructors (TIs), immediately began to yell and scream at us. He ordered us to fall into formation, which nobody at that point had been told how to do, and referred to us as *rainbows* because we still wore our multi-colored civilian clothes.

The TI marched us to the chow hall for breakfast, after which he marched us to an administrative hall known as the White Elephant to complete our paperwork. As he herded us from place to place, the sergeant continued to scream at us using his preferred method for teaching us how to march properly. He'd bring us back to the barracks for ten-to-fifteen minutes. Forbidden to climb in our bunks during the day, we'd lay back on our footlockers and catch a minute or two of sleep. Then, we were off to another destination.

By the end of the day, we were all exhausted. But we did learn a few things from this TI, as we stowed gear in our footlockers that first evening. Sergeant White taught us how to make up two sets of toiletries.[2] One set was never to be used. It contained a shiny new razor, a toothbrush that had never touched a tooth, and a tube of toothpaste that had never been squeezed. This pristine set of toiletries was kept in our footlockers for inspection by Sergeant White

---

2　These sets did not contain combs because we got our heads shaved weekly, and there was never enough hair to comb.

and the other TIs. The second set we stowed in a plastic bag behind a wall panel. We used this latter set to shave in the morning and to brush our teeth in the evening, after the sergeant returned to his office. The bottom line—it was impossible to get our "everyday" set clean enough to pass inspection.

At first we'd march for most of the day. Our TIs grouped us into flights. Out on the drill pad, ten-to-twelve flights marched at the same time. Each flight's TI would walk with them. Sergeant White shouted each of our names, and we'd learn how to properly leave the rank and file, salute, and report to him. I was the first to be called out. I'd face him, salute, and shout, "Sir. Airman Basic Schwerman Ronald L. reporting as ordered, sir!" Back in the rank and file, the TI peered at me from under his drab olive green utility cap and barked his first words of encouragement, "Schwerman, you did a good job."

From the beginning of boot camp, we received training in field skills like how to build a toilet in the woods and how to survive a gas attack. On one occasion, we were each issued a gas mask and told to wear it into a big room. Then Sergeant White entered the room without a mask and instructed us to take ours off. We did, and immediately realized the room was filled with tear gas that burned our eyes. It was terrible, but the TI wasn't bothered by it.[3] From this, we learned two valuable lessons: things aren't always as

---

3 Apparently the TI had developed some immunity to the tear gas which was issuing from a single lit candle in the room.

they seem, and we should respect those with higher rank and longevity (like the TI) who knew things we recruits didn't know.

We also trained with the M1 rifle. After two-to-three weeks of practice, we had to qualify with the M1. This involved both firing the rifle and learning how to launch grenades with it. I had never fired a rifle in my life, but I did pretty well. Marching somewhere the day after our qualifying rounds, Sergeant White halted our flight and put us at ease. "Schwerman," he said, directing his attention to me. "I've got a question for you."

"Sir! Yes, sir." I responded.

"I didn't know you had rifles in Minnesota," he continued.

"Sir! Yes, we do, sir!" I replied.

"Because," the TI continued, "you shot almost a perfect score." I knew before entering the Air Force that I had good vision. I could read a license plate half block away. What I learned from this exercise was that I also had the ability to take instruction on how to stand, how to breathe, and how to sight the rifle, and I'd hit the bull's-eye almost every time. That little bit of recognition by Sergeant White gave me a sense of accomplishment that propelled me through even the toughest experiences of boot camp. These included guard duty (at one point, I was assigned to guard a tree) and KP, at which all airmen took turns. The days we pulled KP, the barracks guard woke us at 0400 and we'd fall back into our bunks around 2100 that night—dusty, greasy, and dog tired.

Besides the field training, we attended school at Lackland. There were no classes yet in aircraft operation or maintenance. It was all basic rules, regulations, and procedures you needed to know just to function in the U.S. Air Force.

The subjects we studied were as diverse as the Uniform Code of Military Justice, the history of war, and how to avoid sexually transmitted diseases. They were teaching us the basics of life, as young kids who had just left home and were now out in the world with the Air Force as their daddy.

A few days after arriving at Lackland for boot camp, I got so sick that I was given permission by our TI to go on sick call. I remember having to take a towel, a toothbrush, and some other toiletries with me to the base clinic in case I was hospitalized. At the clinic, the doctor gave me a shot in my butt and prescribed twenty-four hours of bed rest. I was allowed to return to my barracks, and within hours I began feeling better. When the TI came into the barracks that evening, I was up and walking around. He chewed me out for not being in bed, but I was all right the next day. I might have had a bug, but it was mainly exhaustion.

I was a smoker, and for the first few weeks of boot camp we weren't allowed to smoke. In retrospect, this would have been a good time to quit, but I didn't. Those of us who were smokers would sneak cigarettes when Sergeant White was out of the barracks. We'd go into the bathroom where there was a fan and blow smoke out of the window. After a while, we were once again allowed to smoke openly.

We marched over to the laundry one evening and were at ease in line when the sergeant told us "the smoking lamp is lit." The smokers pulled out cigarettes. I was standing there puffing away and daydreaming, when I looked up and saw my flight marching away from me. I ran to get in my place and managed to do it without being spotted, but all of a sudden I realized I had a lit cigarette in my hand. Before I could stow it, Sergeant White saw the cigarette, and ordered me to report to his office when we got back to the barracks. I was scared to death.

There was a line of guys who had to report. Each of us knew the drill: knock once, wait for permission to enter, and open the door. When my turn came, I stepped inside and yelled, "Sir! Airman Basic Schwerman Ronald L reporting as ordered, sir!" "Close the door, airman!" barked the sergeant. Then he began chewing me out. At the same time, he began slamming chairs around the room. To the line of guys waiting outside his door, it sounded like he was beating me up. He wasn't, but I think he did it to put fear in their hearts of what was coming for each of them.

In the end, I got a gig (a demerit) for my inappropriate behavior. If you earned enough gigs, it would set you back and you might have to start boot camp all over again. As far as I can remember, that was the only gig I received.

Everything we did in basic training involved strict discipline. At meal times, we'd grab the food trays on both sides and hold them vertically in front of our chests while standing at attention. Then, we'd march sideways in the chow line, slap our trays down on the counter and put dishes on them. The kitchen staff would heap all the food we could eat on our dishes, and we'd walk to the tables, standing at attention until there were four people at each. We wouldn't eat until everyone who wanted to pray got to pray. We were all tired, scared and homesick. I think we all prayed—even the atheists.

GROUND POWER SCHOOL AT CHANUTE

About four weeks into basic training, I received orders for Keesler Air Force Base in Biloxi, Mississippi, where I was to attend autopilot school. In this tech school, I'd learn how to repair and diagnose problems with the system that flies the plane when the pilot is not manually controlling the aircraft.

I was delighted with my assignment. First off, it was really up my alley because it was mostly electronics. Second, it was a good, long school. By the time I finished the eighteen-month autopilot course, I would only have a couple years left in my Air Force enlistment. As new as I was to the military, I had already decided I didn't want to make it a career. But there was one more reason I was happy about my assignment. Biloxi was close to New Orleans, which I considered a party city. Unfortunately (or perhaps fortunately) this assignment was not to be.

Before leaving for Biloxi, I was given an eye exam and the technician discovered I was colorblind. This resulted in a change of orders from autopilot school in Mississippi to aerospace ground equipment school in Illinois. I was to report to Chanute Air Force Base in Rantoul, Illinois, for the remaining two weeks of my basic training and wait there to enter the next six-month course in maintenance and repair of equipment used to provide power, heating, cooling, and hydraulics to aircraft while on the ground.

Part of my job involved maintaining the compressors used to start jet aircraft by shooting a stream of air directly into the turbine. Like blowing on the blades of a fan, this stream of air caused the turbine to begin turning. Once it was turning at about 35 percent of rotation, fuel squirted into the combustion chamber, a spark lit the fuel, and the engine fired up. We also maintained the generator sets used to start propeller-driven planes still in use because of their ability to come in slowly over a target.

The course wasn't entirely electronic. I would also learn hydraulics, pneumatics, and other engineering disciplines needed to repair the machines collectively referred to as ground power equipment.

Discipline was tougher at Chanute. Appearance was ten times as hard as boot camp. The men of our 3360 School Squadron had to shine their shoes, and starch and press their clothes every night, in preparation for inspection the following day.

Each of us had a morning job. Mine was latrine queen. I loved my job because it took only an hour, and after I finished I could do what I wanted until inspection. Besides cleaning the place, I had to set up big buckets containing heavy plastic bags. Everyone was told to urinate in those buckets in the morning. Later, a truck would come by and pick up those bags of morning urine. The urine was used, so we were told, to make blood thinners at the local hospital.[4]

---

4   A possible reference to the isolation of urokinase, which is produced in the kidney, voided in the urine and used to dissolve blood clots.

Following this morning ritual, no one was allowed to use the latrine until it passed inspection, which occurred around 1000 hours.

First, the barracks was inspected while we stood at attention by our bunks. Next, we fell out in front of the squadron office for personal inspection. Our faces had to be cleanly shaved, our fatigues could not have creases in the elbows or knees, and our shoes had to be polished just so. If our personal appearance was not satisfactory, we received demerits, so we learned how to do everything with perfection.

Take shoe shining, for instance. We'd apply a thick coat of shoe polish, then using a candle or a Zippo lighter, we'd hold a flame to the polish. We'd do that over and over to build up a base. It was a long, hard process, but it paid off in the long run. With the base in place, all we had to do was to apply a thin layer of polish and buff our shoes with a wet cotton ball and cold water to achieve a shine resembling patent leather. It only took about twenty minutes a night.

We attended school from 1200 to 1800 hours each weekday, marching to and from these classes. At the end of the day, we marched to chow. Finally, dismissed from formation, we walked back to the barracks to study and shine our shoes all over again. We fell out for inspection every weekday, but we were free on weekends.

Despite my disappointment at being cut from autopilot school, life was good at Chanute. I went to school, worked hard, and didn't get into any major problems. Rantoul was a small rural town just fifteen miles north of the University of Illinois at Champaign-Urbana. My buddies and I visited the university a couple of times but spent most of our free time at the base restaurant where you could buy beer and food. I continued my drinking in tech school, but because of our rigorous schedule I pretty much stayed out of trouble. Every Sunday morning I would wake to the ringing of a church bell just a half-block away. I never considered going, though, as I was often hung over.

My studies kept me very busy, but I did miss Judie. We kept in touch by letter, and five months after joining the Air Force, I was granted my first leave to return to Minneapolis to visit both my girlfriend and my family.

CIRCUMSTANCES BEYOND MY CONTROL

While at Chanute, I formed a lifelong friendship with a Cleveland-born airman, Cliff Thielman. The Cleveland Indians offered Cliff, then a high school shortstop, a signing bonus. Instead, he enlisted in the U.S. Air Force with the dream of becoming a pilot. Like me, vision problems sent Cliff to tech school instead. In many ways, Cliff and I were opposites. I avoided leadership while he sought it, becoming a Green Rope in our barracks.[5] I drank heavily and Cliff didn't drink at all, perhaps because of the abuse he suffered at the hands of an alcoholic stepfather. Despite our differ-

---

5   **Green Ropes** – Also referred to as Bay Chiefs or Element Leaders, these motivated students volunteer to be responsible for all airmen assigned to a dormitory bay and/or element, including marching them to and from class. Ron Powers, "Air Force Technical School Restrictions." http://usmilitary.about.com/od/airforcejoin/a/ropes.htm

ences, we became fast friends. "You were always so carefree and fun to be around," Cliff would tell me years later. From my perspective, Cliff kept me grounded.

I was at Chanute a total of seven months—one month to finish boot camp and wait for the next AGE class to start, and six months to complete the course. Toward the end of tech school, I filled out my dream sheet, ranking the three places I most wanted to go: Duluth, Minnesota; Germany; and California. When I received orders to my Permanent Change of Station a few weeks later, I learned that I had been granted my first choice. I would report to the Air Defense Command, 30th Air Division as part of the Consolidated Aircraft Maintenance Squadron 343rd, stationed at the Duluth Air Base. "I'm going to Duluth," I told my friend Cliff. "If you ever get that way, let me know. Let's stay in touch." One week after I left Chanute, Cliff Thielman and a few others from my class received orders for Duluth as well.

What happened between tech school and my arrival at Duluth might have served as a warning of what was to come, if I had been paying closer attention to world events. It was just before 1300 hours, 22 November 1963, and I was home on leave in Minneapolis, sleeping off a hangover in the bedroom I'd occupied since I was six years old. Mom entered my room visibly shaken. "Ronald, wake up!" she said. "They shot President Kennedy."

Owing to the proximity of the assassination to the Cuban Missile Crisis, just over one year before, the military went on red alert as authorities tried to determine whether it had been carried out by another country. This tragic event, with worldwide repercussions, underlined how little control I had as an Airman Second Class over forces that would ultimately shape my life. I was caught in the undertow.

CHAPTER 5

Caught in the Undertow

DULUTH AIR BASE

My orders instructed me to be at my Permanent Change of Station by 3 December 1963, so I took an evening train the 150 miles north, arriving in Duluth around 2100 hours. It was dark and snowing hard when we pulled into the depot. My orders gave me a phone number to call on arrival, and the Air Force would send someone to pick me up. I walked down Superior Street through swirls of white and found a restaurant still open. After making my call at the pay phone, I took a seat at the counter, ordered a cup of coffee, and waited for my ride.

The mission of the Duluth Air Base was to defend against attack from Russian bombers over the North Pole. We had eight F106 Delta Darts, each carrying a nuclear warhead, on alert at all times. If we had to take our aircraft off alert for exercise, another base would cover for us. The Duluth Air Base was part of the Pinetree Line of bases with ground-to-air and air-to-air defenses that guarded the northern perimeter of the United States along the 50th parallel, from Washington State to Maine.

The Distant Early Warning (DEW) Line, an array of radar stations to the north along the Arctic Circle, transmitted signals back to the Pinetree Line. At Duluth, these signals were received in the SAGE[1] building, named for the system it contained for tracking and intercepting enemy bombers. Unauthorized personnel, including Air Force personnel without clearance, were not allowed near that place under threat of being shot. If Russia attacked, signals from the DEW line would be received in the SAGE building, putting our F106s in the air and guiding them to their menacing targets.

My job at the Duluth Air Base was maintenance and repair of ground power equipment required by the F106s and other aircraft on the ground.

DEFINITELY NO FAMILY MAN

When I filled out my dream sheet, I might have picked Germany or even sunny California as my first preference, but I chose a lo-

---

1   **SAGE** – Semi-Automatic Ground Environment

cation close to home. The U.S. Air Force obliged. Stationed just three hours north of Minneapolis, I could ride the train home on weekends, drink with my friends, and see my girl.

I was committed to Judie, but not exclusively. In fact, from the very hour I arrived in Duluth, I began to be unfaithful. Waiting at the restaurant for my ride to the base, I struck up a conversation with a waitress named Jean, and we began dating. We'd see each other during the week, and I'd spend my weekends with Judie. I was a two-timer.

There was no sexual relationship with Jean; that was her choice, not mine. We'd just go out and talk. But sex was definitely a part of my life with Judie. On weekends, I stayed at Judie's apartment in Minneapolis and partied. During the week, I lived in a barracks for single airman on the Duluth Air Force Base.

My friend Cliff lived downtown Duluth with his wife Nancy and their newborn baby boy, Gary. So it seemed a little unusual that, one cold and windy evening in early 1964, Cliff knocked on the door of my second-floor room at the barracks. "I've got a problem with my car," he said. "Can you come down and help me fix it?" He led me downstairs to the blue and white '56 Chevy I helped him buy from an old lady in Bloomington, Minnesota, just a month or two before. Cliff had the hood open and was standing in front of the engine. "Go around and try to start it," he urged, so I went around to the driver's side and got in. To my surprise, there was Judie. "What are you doing here?" I exclaimed. We kissed and then Judie whispered, "I've got something to tell you!"

"What?" I asked. "I'm pregnant," she said, with a half smile. Realizing she had missed her period, she decided take the train to Duluth and deliver the news in person. She asked Cliff and Nancy to pick her up at the depot and set up this elaborate ruse. "Are you surprised?" she wondered.

Dumbfounded was a better word. The idea of having a child signaled a whole new phase in life, for which I was decidedly unprepared. But in those days you didn't abort babies, and if you got a girl pregnant, generally you married her. So we began planning our wedding, which took place on 26 May 1964 at Trinity First Lutheran Church in Minneapolis.

At first Judie and I rented a small apartment at 822 East Fifth Street in Duluth. That was where we lived when our first daughter, Pam, was born 25 December 1964. Besides the tiny living space, which seemed even smaller with the addition of our newborn daughter, we had some problems with the landlord. He wasn't providing the heat we needed to keep our newborn baby warm, so in the spring of 1965, we moved.

This time, we moved in with an elderly Jewish man named Sam who rented part of his house to us. I would go down to the lake and catch northern pike for him. He loved the fish and would give us steak in return. He could also make a delicious liver pâté. Sam knew how to cook and eat.

We got along well with our new landlord, but it would not be a long-term relationship. Judie was already pregnant again. We had informed Sam of this before we moved in, and he seemed okay with it.

But as the due date approached, our 80-year-old host began to have difficulty with the thought of two small children living in his house.

So in the fall of 1965, we moved to a spacious third floor apartment at 1905 East Superior Street in Duluth. It was owned by a soon-to-be-retired Air Force NCO who rented it to us for only sixty-dollars a month. I recall carrying our washing machine upstairs with some difficulty to the third floor, but this apartment was wonderful. Located right on Lake Superior, we could hear the foghorns as they warned ships off the rocks. On 17 November 1965 Judie gave birth to our second daughter, Rhonda.

While Judie and I lived together in Duluth as a legally married couple with one and then two daughters, that does not mean I had changed my ways. I was definitely not a family man. We had friends like Cliff and Nancy that we'd have dinner or coffee with from time to time. But my friendship with Cliff was primarily at work. I filled my off-hours with other friends that liked to party.

Although he wasn't a drunk like I had become, my supervisor Sergeant Cobb was a drinking buddy. We'd bar-hop all over the county. One night he drove me back to the apartment so inebriated that I fell on my face as I walked in the door. I was scheduled to work at 2300 hours, so I told Judie to call Sergeant Cobb and tell him I wasn't coming in. She did, and of course he didn't say anything because I had been out drinking with him.

Besides being a drunk, I was totally unfaithful to Judie. I had affairs with at least three women while we lived in Duluth. It was one thing for me to be chasing around with other women while

I was single, which was in itself dishonest, but it was another to continue drinking and chasing other women when I was married and had two children.

I paid the bills and kept my family fed and clothed, but I was not a good husband or father. Looking back on this time in my life, I am filled with shame at the way I acted. I do not think I was capable of loving Judie as a husband should love his wife. Part of me wanted a relationship with my wife, but part of me wanted my freedom. Too many things like booze and other women were more important than her. I was just in the marriage because this is where I had to be.

As far as I know, Judie never knew what was going on behind her back. She was a good wife and mother, and she was not particularly concerned about my drinking. As far as she was concerned, I just went to bed and slept it off. In fact, I was well on my way to becoming an alcoholic.

Judie did get irritated when I left her alone to go drinking. Once when she and I had plans to go out together, a friend of mine named Rich called and offered to take me for a ride in his Mustang. Without asking Judie, I accepted. When she found out, she was upset. On my way out the door, Judie kicked me squarely in the butt. I turned and pushed her down on the couch. "Don't you ever do a thing like that again," I warned her. Then I left for a few beers and a joyride in Dick's brand new Ford. Wherever I went, with or without Judie, alcohol played a big part in my life.

Despite earlier conversations about making a Christian home, religion played no part in our lives in those early years. We never prayed, read the Bible, or went to church. I guess I just never thought very far out. We lived one day at a time, and neither of us was ready for marriage or to raise a family.

THE WORLD AND MY LIFE CONVERGE

While I worked at the Duluth Air Force Base and played at marriage, a worldwide spark that had been smoldering for years grew hotter and finally burst into flame.

The Soviet Union overran Eastern Europe at the end of World War II, and budding Marxist revolutions in Asia, Africa, and South America (too close to home) resulted in East and West squaring off against each other at several points around the globe. Trying to avoid another world war but determined to contain the Communist threat, the U.S. butted heads with the U.S.S.R. and China in conflicts like the Korean War, where my brother LeRoy served.

Even closer to home, as I completed my junior year in high school, CIA-trained Cuban exiles attempted a counter-revolution and were rebuffed by the Soviet-educated army of Communist dictator Fidel Castro at the infamous Bay of Pigs Invasion—just over a hundred miles southeast of Key West, Florida.

As I graduated from high school and began post-graduate electronics school, the U.S. was committing more and more civilian and military advisors to another third-world region where we were determined to make a stand against Marxism—Vietnam in Southeast Asia.

A French colony before World War II, Vietnam was divided into two countries by a 1954 agreement of the superpowers. In the early

60s, the U.S. found itself in the distasteful, though necessary, position of bolstering a dictatorship in South Vietnam in its struggle against Communist North Vietnam and its sponsors, Russia and China.

By the time our first daughter was born in December 1964, North Vietnam had attacked a U.S. warship, and President Lyndon Johnson had secured from the U.S. Congress a resolution giving him authority to take military action.

By the time our second daughter was born less than one year later, the U.S. had begun a bombing campaign called Operation Rolling Thunder against select North Vietnamese targets, and the first U.S. Marines had arrived to defend the U.S. air base at Da Nang, South Vietnam. The number of troops committed to the conflict escalated rapidly. At the end of 1964, there were approximately 23,000 Americans in Vietnam; by the end of 1965, the U.S. personnel count was about 200,000; and by the end of 1966, U.S. forces had risen to nearly 365,000.[2] I was to be one of them.

WAR TURNS REAL

I opened my orders to Vietnam in February 1966. Before receiving my orders, the escalating conflict in Southeast Asia wasn't even on my radar. On 2 March 1965, I remember watching President Johnson on TV as he announced the beginning of Operation Rolling Thunder. For the past year, I'd followed the build-up of troops. I even looked

---

2   Andrew A. Wiest, *Essential Histories: The Vietnam War, 1956-1975*, (Great Brittain: Osprey Publishing, 2002).

at pictures one airman brought back of the bodies of Viet Cong that had been killed right outside a base where he was stationed.

I thought about this, the fighting going on half a world away. But I didn't take it personally until that day in early February when the head of our shop, Sergeant Wert, walked over and handed envelopes to a few of us. Here they were: my orders to Phan Rang, Vietnam. I was instructed to report at Travis Air Force Base near San Francisco and fly from there to Vietnam via commercial airliner. We were sent separately, but several of us, including my good friend Cliff Thielman, would ship out together from Travis because we had the same orders.

I just didn't know what to expect from this new development in my life. I knew it was war, and people were going to be dying. I was scared to death, so I approached the departure date in the only way I knew how—I did a lot more drinking.

Curiously, there was one guy in our ground power equipment shop in Duluth who tried to offer himself instead of me. He thought it was unfair that a married man with children would be ordered to Vietnam. He broached the subject with Sergeant Wert who told him flatly, "No, you can't go for Schwerman."

I give him credit for his courage. He just wanted to be a good guy, but he was much younger than me, and the fact that I had more stripes probably weighed against his argument. At that point, the U.S. Air Force needed people in Vietnam with a little more experience. If it had been up to me, I probably would have let him go in my place.

CHAPTER 6

My Year in Vietnam

MINNEAPOLIS INTERNATIONAL AIRPORT

FEBRUARY 1966

My orders to Vietnam had arrived while I was stationed at Duluth, Minnesota. The Air Force granted me a thirty-day leave prior to my deployment. I used part of that time to move Judie and the kids to Minneapolis. Then, I boarded a commercial airliner at Twin Cities' International for a flight to San Francisco. I was scheduled to attend a two-week training school at Hamilton Air Force Base before shipping out to Southeast Asia.

Sitting on the plane at the Charles Lindberg Terminal just prior to take-off, I recall looking out the window and feeling very alone. I had just said goodbye to my daughters and my dad in the terminal building. Judie and I hugged and kissed, but nothing else was said. It was a scary feeling, and I don't think either of us knew what I was in for. As turbines began to rotate and my family waved one more time before my plane left the gate, it seemed like we were separated by more than a few yards and two panes of glass.

It was dark when we landed on the west coast. I took a bus from the airport to downtown San Francisco. It would be a few days before I needed to report for training at Hamilton AFB, so I grabbed a room at the YMCA and walked around the city. In keeping with my self-centered nature, I squandered these days at the end of my leave to see the sights and engage in more drinking instead of spending time with Judie and the kids.

During my stay in San Francisco, I met a female Marine fresh out of boot camp. We did a little partying together, in her room or mine. No sex was involved—we just drank and talked. I tipped a few more glasses with an Army infantryman from Fort Ord. Then I caught a bus to Hamilton AFB, thirty miles north of the Golden Gate Bridge, and finally reported for duty.

In training school, we learned to operate an M-16 rifle and an M-60 7.62 mm machine gun. Boards would pop up depicting a VC Charlie (the enemy), a papa-san (an older Vietnamese man) or a mama-san (an older Vietnamese woman). We had to quickly decide whether or not to shoot. If a Charlie popped up, we had better shoot fast or be shot. If we shot at a papa-san or a mama-san, we shot too fast and had just killed a civilian. It was a reminder that real people would soon be shooting at us with real bullets.

As part of our jungle combat training, we also practiced surviving a mustard gas attack (not the real stuff) and throwing grenades (that were real). After finishing my training, I rode a bus to Travis Air Force Base where I would board a 707 with old friends like Cliff from Duluth and new friends made at Hamilton. Our flight to Vietnam, operated by Trans World Airlines, would span twenty-three hours and include stops in Hawaii and the Philippines.

Waiting to board the commercial airliner, I met an Air Force chaplain. "I sure am glad to be Air Force instead of Army infantry," he said. Having just finished jungle combat training, I readily agreed. Our support role on heavily guarded air bases was considered much less dangerous than patrolling enemy infested jungles. But as we would soon learn, death stalked the runways of Vietnam as well.

REAL PEOPLE SHOOT REAL BULLETS

At 1800 hours on 10 March 1966 I recorded my first impressions of Vietnam as I walked down the airstairs of the TWA Boeing 707 and onto the asphalt parking apron at Tan Son Nhut Air Base. To my skin, the air felt terribly hot and muggy.[1] Everything I set my eyes on was a drab grey or olive-green. There was no color anywhere. Stress, on the other hand, was everywhere on the faces of those deplaning and those receiving us. But it was with my nose that I recorded my most vivid first impression. Vietnam smelled of

---

1   Many days during my tour in Vietnam the temperature exceeded 100° F. Air temperatures of 100°-120° F were not unusual.

death—or blood. It was depressing just knowing I had to be here for a year and wondering if I'd make it out alive.

Our landing in Vietnam hinted at the rapidly escalating war to which we were soon inserted. Instead of a normal glide path and a steady drop to the ground, the pilot had put our commercial airliner into a steep dive and pulled out just before touching the runway. As I later learned, this was standard procedure for aircraft operating in a war zone where the Viet Cong[2] fired rifles, mortars, and later rockets at flights landing or taking off, regardless of whether they were military or civilian.

It was late Wednesday afternoon, 10 March 1966 when we landed at Tan Son Nhut, just outside of Saigon. Entering the terminal, my traveling companions and I met up with some Australian infantrymen who had also just arrived. We sat together, drinking beer and commiserating. We were new, they were new, and we had something else in common—we were all scared, not knowing what lay ahead.

Our original orders had us stationed at Phan Rang Air Base. Located a hundred miles northeast of Saigon, the former French airfield had been rebuilt by the United States the year before. At Phan Rang, my buddy Cliff and I would join up with the Field Maintenance Squadron (FMS) from Holloman AFB at Alamogordo, New

---

2   Members of the National Liberation Front, a political and military organization supported by North Vietnam and its allies that fought the South Vietnam government, the U.S. military and other allies of South Vietnam from 1954 to 1976.

Mexico to provide support to the 366th Tactical Fighter Wing—the first permanent USAF organization to be stationed there.

Within two days of arriving in Vietnam, however, we learned we would be reissued orders to Da Nang Air Base.

Awaiting these new orders, we stayed at Tan Son Nhut in dusty old World War II tents whose strong smelling canvas burned my sinuses. We spent most of our time sleeping, eating at the chow hall, and writing letters. On a couple of occasions, we ventured to downtown Saigon, the bustling capital of South Vietnam. Its streets were flooded with thousands and thousands of people—older Vietnamese carrying poles with baskets at the ends and young kids on scooters, the preferred transportation. Downtown streets were paved, but streets on the outskirts of town were dirt. Dust filled the air from all the traffic. Back on base, the Air Force required us to report once each day in formation to confirm we were alive and hadn't gone AWOL.

Two weeks after arriving in Vietnam, I finally received my orders to Da Nang Air Base, 400 miles north of Saigon and just eighty-five miles from the demilitarized zone separating South Vietnam from the Communist North. Geographically, I was being sent into the heart of the conflict.

FIRST DAYS AT DA NANG

After two weeks in Vietnam, Cliff and I boarded a C-130 Hercules four-engine turboprop for the flight to Da Nang Air Base where I would spend almost one year. Back in the States, I had watched a newsreel of the Marines' landing at Da Nang and taking over this former French air base the previous March. It was an amphibious landing meant to showcase the arrival of the first U.S. combat forces in Vietnam.

Arriving at Da Nang, we spent the first two days walking around the base with our paperwork, getting to know the layout, exchanging our U.S. dollars for Military Payment Certificates or Vietnamese piastre, and collecting the personal items we needed to live there for a year. Since we came from a cold climate, we needed clothes that would allow us to function in the tropical heat and humidity of Southeast Asia. The Air Force also issued us tools for our work and identification for the chow hall. Each of us received a Geneva Card. If captured, we were to give the enemy our name, rank and serial number, and show them our Geneva Cards which told them how they were to treat us.

Finally, we went to our shop, found out what our job was, and met the people we'd be working with. Most of the people in my shop came from the 366 FMS based in New Mexico. The non-commissioned officer-in-charge (NCOIC) of our shop was a senior master sergeant with the last name of Meyer. He was a short, stocky guy with brown hair. Our shop also had an administrative officer named Captain Anderson. In addition we had many NCOs. I was an E4 (a buck sergeant) and I had met another NCO, Sergeant Stafford, on the plane to Vietnam. Many of the others I did not know, but we'd soon meet and become friends. Lastly, a handful of men like Cliff Thielman had come with me from Duluth.

My first job was driving dispatch, which involved transporting ground power equipment between our shop and various aircraft. I'd get a radio call from Control: "Rainbow 2, we need a MA-1A gas turbine compressor."[3] I'd locate the equipment, hitch it to whatever I was driving, take it to where it was needed, and park it in position. It might be an air compressor to start the aircraft or a test stand used for maintenance and service of an aircraft's hydraulic system, or it might be an air conditioner which providing cooling for planes on the ground as technicians ran the radar or electronics.

If someone called from the flight line to say an air compressor they were using didn't work, I'd bring them another and pick up the malfunctioning equipment. I didn't do any equipment repair at the beginning, only minor maintenance. If equipment was broken down, I'd usually take it to the main shop where mechanics with more experience would repair it.

There were three or four of us driving dispatch on the flight line twenty-four hours a day, divided into three shifts. I worked days when I got there, but over the next year I would work all of the shifts. I enjoyed the evening or night shifts best, because the high-ranking officers weren't around.

I did occasionally work twelve-hour shifts, if there were a lot of equipment breakdowns or if there was unusually heavy fighting and the planes were flying more often. When there was no flying

---

3 Rainbow 1, 2, 3, etc. identified each tractor being used to deliver equipment to the aircraft.

going on, there was little to do around the shop because the equipment wasn't needed and didn't break.[4]

LIFE ON THE AIR BASE

During my year in Vietnam, we spent our off-duty time in an area of the base that we affectionately and wryly referred to as "Camp Da Nang." We lived in tents for the first ten months, while workers constructed permanent barracks. We slept in double bunks—one above and one below—with twenty guys to a tent. These tents were open around the bottom, so we all slept under mosquito netting because malaria was a real problem. To combat the tropical disease, the Air Force issued anti-malarial drugs and told us to take one pill a week. They gave us extra pills to take when we left Vietnam, because the micro-organism causing the disease can live in the human body up to six weeks.

Working together, the airmen I lived with converted our tent into something resembling a house. We built a porch onto it that even boasted a barber chair. One of our bunkmates, a tall, chatty African-American, was a barber in civilian life. He'd give haircuts for a buck or two a head, and he was very good at it. If he wasn't available or the line to his chair grew too long, we could visit the barbershop in the BX[5] outside the base.

---

4   The U.S. occasionally called truces for holidays or to give peace initiatives a chance. During truces, military aircraft did not fly, reducing the need for ground power equipment.

5   **Base Exchange (BX)** – a retail store operated by the U.S. Air Force on or just off base and providing a place for members of the military to purchase a variety of merchandise for personal use.

When I arrived at Camp Da Nang, all we had for bathing was cold water flowing from a pipe sticking out of the ground. We were told not to drink that water, but we could use it for washing up. After removing the netting from our metal helmets, we filled them with water, shaved and cleaned ourselves as best we could using these improvised basins.

Later, the Air Force built showers. A small water heater located on top of a building fed pipes sticking out of the ceilings. Holes drilled into these straight pipes created a shower effect. There were no stalls; everyone showered together. The first ones in got warm water, but it didn't last long. The rest took cold showers.

With towels wrapped around our waists, we walked the forty-yards back to Camp Da Nang in temperatures often exceeding one-hundred degrees. By the time we got back to our tents, we were covered in dust and sweat so the showers didn't help much. I'm not complaining, though. We were well-off compared to infantrymen patrolling the jungle for ten days or more, without showers and with only C-rations to eat.

We ate C-rations too, and once a week helicopters would fly hot dinners to the infantry. But those of us on base also had a mess hall and each airman was issued a mess kit. Big garbage cans full of water with gas-powered heating elements inside greeted us at the entrance to the hall. We'd dip our mess kits in that boiling water before eating to sterilize them, and we did it religiously because we didn't want to get dysentery. If an airman dropped his mess kit into the water, though, he didn't reach in and get it. The boiling water would scald his hand.

Then we'd go through the chow line and pick up our food. The bread always had some sort of bug in it; we'd just pick that out of our food. But the rest of the meal was usually good—real meat and potatoes.

When the mess hall stoves weren't operating, which happened every ten days for some reason we never did figure out, we had to eat C-rations. Some guys didn't like C-rations, but I did. I kept a box at the end of my bunk and told everyone to throw whatever they didn't want into the box. They'd toss in peanut butter, a can of stew, a package of toilet paper, a pack of three-to-four cigarettes, a can opener, crackers, little cans with cake in them, and so on. Then I or anyone else that wanted to could rummage through the box if we got hungry. It was a community place for everyone to put their discarded C-rations rather than throwing them in the trash.

The Vietnamese people

The first civilians I spied, as I walked down the airway from the 707 that brought me to Southeast Asia, wore black pajama pants all the way to their ankles, full-length sleeves, and hats covering their heads and shoulders.

Spending most of my time on an air base, I had limited contact with the people we were deployed to defend, with a few notable exceptions. I became acquainted with a guy we knew as "Chuck" who came by our tent on a motor scooter once a week to pick up our laundry. This same guy was a helicopter mechanic in the Vietnamese Air Force (the VNAF). We'd pay Chuck for the laundry service and also the mama-san who would sweep the floors in our tent and empty garbage.

I was a smoker, and one morning after pulling a night shift, I made the big mistake of crawling into bed and leaving my cigarettes out. Spying my pack, a mama-san asked if she could have one. "Sure." I said, and promptly fell asleep. From that day on, the mama-sans who cleaned our tents took a break for lunch and helped themselves to my cigarettes. No big thing. We got our smokes free or bought them for as little as ninety-cents a carton. So I didn't care if they pinched my smokes.

One other thing I remember vividly about the mama-sans is that their teeth were black from chewing betel nut which acts as a stimulant similar to tobacco or nicotine.

Some airmen disliked the Vietnamese people. I had nothing against them—in fact I thought they were a great people. I had a friend who was a VNAF pilot, and I liked him. What I didn't like was Americans calling the Vietnamese "gooks." Coming from a Christian background, I was taught that God loves all people.[6]

Problem was, it was hard to tell a friendly South Vietnamese citizen from a Viet Cong. One day, I waited along with other airmen for a bus at the entrance to Camp Da Nang. Every half hour, a

---

6   As I was growing up, I remember my mother saying, "Black people are just as good as us . . ." The unstated ending to that sentence was ". . . as long as they stay in their place and we stay in ours." As much as we professed equity, interracial marriage was a no-no.

blue Air Force bus would come by the gate to take us down to the base compound. That day, a Vietnamese solider and a U.S. solder guarded the gate. As we waited for our ride, a Vietnamese woman came in the gate with her bag. She probably worked there as a mamma-san, cleaning tents. Anyway, the guards stopped her and looked through her bag. I don't know what they found, but suddenly the Vietnamese guard began beating her with the butt of his rifle while the American guard looked on. The guard beat her mercilessly around the head and the body. It was a terrible sight, but those of us waiting for the bus just minded our own business. We weren't going to mess with the guard, first because he had a gun, and second because she might have been Viet Cong.

After hours

At work or off work, I had good friends who helped pass the time while we were stuck in Vietnam. We'd go down to the Airman's Club at the main compound and have a few beers—usually too many. Or we'd stop at one of the small "beer joints" close to Camp Da Nang. Beer was a nickel a can, so for a dollar we could drink to our hearts content.

My interests determined some of my friendships. I tutored and hung out with one airman who had a hard time with electronics. That was part of our job, so I was teaching him the basics.

I got along with everyone pretty well, but there were exceptions. One night, I was drinking with a guy who had had several hundred dollars on him. We got pretty drunk and somehow he couldn't find the money. He accused me of stealing it, and we wrestled, knocking over tables and generally tearing up our tent. At one point, we ripped up the bed and locker of a fellow airman, who jumped into the fight on my side. Thankfully, nobody got hurt, and the guy who started it came back the next morning to apologize. After sobering up, he remembered where he put his money.

Another time I got into a row with Sergeant Stafford, who I met on the plane to Vietnam. Cliff and I had decided to visit one of the places on the base where the girls were. Blue Hawaii, as it was called, was a house of prostitution; but it was also a good place to relax and have a beer. So we dressed in civilian clothes and got ready to leave camp.

As we exited our tent, Stafford, who outranked me,[7] asked, "Where are you going?" I said, "We're going to have a beer."

"No, you're not," he insisted. "You're going to start digging foxholes around the tent. We have intelligence that says a mortar attack is coming."

The sergeant had always struck me as a tough guy who was proud of his training in jungle warfare, but at that point I was in no mood for his bluster and puffery. Besides, the Air Force had printed posters and displayed them all over the base warning us that unless we heard from headquarters, we shouldn't be spreading rumors that we were having an attack. So I squared off with Sergeant Stafford and refused his order.

---

7   Stafford was a staff sergeant with four stripes. I was a buck sergeant with only three.

"No, I'm not coming back and digging foxholes," I said. "I'm going out to have a beer—period!" That's when the sergeant said he would kill me.

Despite his threat, Cliff and I left for the Blue Hawaii. I drank more than a few beers and returned to camp to sleep them off. Next morning, a friend and fellow airman named Gillespie parked a pickup in front of my tent and shook me awake. "You're in trouble Schwerman," he said, through the fog of my hangover. "Get your clothes on and come with me." Sergeant Stafford had reported me for disobeying an order, and the brass told Gillespie to come and get me.

"We're all on your side," said my friend, trying to encourage me as we approached the shop. Nobody liked Stafford, but that did not make a whole lot of difference in the military. I had refused the order of a sergeant who outranked me.

When we arrived, our NCOIC, Sergeant Meyers, was waiting for me along with Captain Andersen and Sergeant Stafford. Sergeant Meyers did most of the talking. He informed me that Sergeant Stafford had reported me for insubordination. "Is this true?" asked the NCOIC.

"Yes, I did disobey him," I admitted. Then I made my defense, "I didn't think we should be digging foxholes since we had no word of an attack from headquarters, and we have been told not to spread rumors."

"You did it wrong," declared Sergeant Meyers. "You should have obeyed him, and then come to see me." That's when I revealed that

Sergeant Stafford had threatened to kill me. What I said lit the NCOIC's fuse. He launched into a verbal tirade against Sergeant Stafford, while I got off with a light reprimand. I had a cool relationship with Stafford for the rest of our time in Vietnam.

DETACHING FROM HOME AND REALITY

During the entire time I was stationed in Vietnam, my family and I depended on the U.S. military mail to keep in contact. Letters to and from Vietnam took about a week each way. My relationship with Judie—never the best when I was there in person—deteriorated even further at a distance of 8,000 miles.

We did have a Military Auxiliary Radio System (MARS) station at the Da Nang Air Base. MARS was an organization of ham radio operators who worked with the military to connect servicemen oversees with their families. A ham operator at Da Nang would connect with an operator in the United States, who would patch us into the phone system. If the call was local, the serviceman didn't have to pay for it.

Once, I stood in line to use the MARS station, but I became so nervous waiting that I left before reaching the operator. It was the same with a tape recorder I tried to use once, just to say hi to my wife and kids. I got so scared thinking about making a cassette tape that I couldn't do it. All kinds of emotions welled up inside me, and I didn't want any of my emotions to show.

So I turned to alcohol to suppress my feelings. I didn't know how to handle fear or sadness properly, but if I swallowed enough booze it was easy to talk and express myself—usually in the wrong way.

One night I snuck off base and went drinking at a local bar with a Marine and a Navy guy. The sailor was part of a special outfit, so he carried an automatic weapon. The Marine had a rifle.

I was pretty drunk and stepped outside to pee. Before I knew it, I was surrounded by unfriendly locals and in big trouble. Out of nowhere my drinking buddies appeared with guns raised and rescued me. They brought me back to the bar and told me how stupid I was to wander off alone. "If you do that again, we'll probably find you in a rice paddy next morning with a knife between your shoulder blades," advised the Navy guy.

Another night I got so mindlessly drunk that I climbed a barbed wire fence along the perimeter of Camp Da Nang and walked alone into a field. In the middle of that field I got sick. I sat down on a rock and started to vomit. All of a sudden, I heard a growl. I turned my head and locked eyes with a German shepherd. Then I realized a rifle was pointed at my head. It was an Air Policeman patrolling the perimeter of our base. "What are you doing out here!" he demanded. When I did not answer, he walked me back to the fence and showed me an opening I could squeeze through.

"Get back to your tent!" he barked. Looking over my shoulder as I stumbled away, I recall seeing triangle shaped signs all along the fence warning *Min*—the Vietnamese word for land mine. I had been wandering through one of our own minefields. The sad thing was that I knew it.[8]

On another occasion, I got so drunk I woke up vomiting all over myself. Friends like Cliff, who admired my carefree attitude, could see the toll my drinking was taking on me inside and out. As he told me later, "I overlooked the drinking because I didn't know how to change you." Nor would I have listened to his advice.

Another friend, an NCO named Marvin, dared to suggest I might have a problem with alcohol. Marvin and I played chess from time to time. In late 1966, he was diagnosed with cancer and sent to the Philippines for further testing. I walked him out to the flight line the day he left Vietnam. While waiting for his plane, he confronted me.

"Ron, you should talk to somebody about your drinking," Marvin said as he got ready to board his flight. "It's getting out of control."

Looking back I can see that my friend was older and wiser. Compared to him, I was a twenty-three-year old kid. Maybe he had some experience with alcoholism—I don't know. Regrettably I didn't take his advice seriously. Alcohol was an important social and coping mechanism, and I still didn't think it affected me negatively.

Nor did I believe my personal unfaithfulness would have a negative affect on my family. After all, I was a male confined to

---

8   A therapist later suggested that I intentionally wandered into a minefield as a way of taking control. All of us lived in mortal fear that the VC might, at any moment, lob a mortar over the perimeter and blow us up.

a war zone. Why shouldn't I satisfy my sexual needs, as long as I was discrete?

Much of the ground power equipment at Da Nang was new to me, so the Air Force sent two other airmen and me to school at Clark Air Force Base in the Philippines for two weeks. Our classes lasted from 0600-to-1200 hours. We were free for the rest of the day. We'd go drinking in the downtown bars and girls would try to pick us up. Occasionally they succeeded.

During my stay in the Philippines, I hooked up with a singer. She asked me if I was temporary duty (TDY) or permanent change of station (PCS). She wanted a boyfriend who was going to be there for several months. I lied and told her I was PCS. I went to her house, not far from the base, and was unfaithful to my wife.

Another time in Vietnam, I went off base and spent a night with a girl. I think we smoked opium that night.

On top of my alcohol dependence and growing detachment from my family, I began to believe the war itself wasn't being fought right. Our hands were tied and the enemy knew it.

CHAPTER 7

Days Leading to Attack

DA NANG AIR BASE VIETNAM

On 2 March 1965, America made a major commitment of aircraft to the Vietnam conflict with the launch of a bombing campaign known as *Operation Rolling Thunder* against a limited list of North Vietnamese targets, in an effort to dissuade the North's support of the Viet Cong insurgency. The first U.S. combat troops arrived at Da Nang on 8 March 1965 to guard the air base against Viet Cong retaliation for these daily air raids.

Over the next year, as more troops arrived and both sides engaged in battle, it became clear that the U.S. would fight a limited war, due to opposition at home and fear of drawing China and Russia into the fight. It also became apparent that the Viet Cong and Communist North Vietnam would fight a guerrilla war—

striking U.S. and ARVN positions and then retreating, often into Cambodia or Laos, to regroup and strike again.[1]

Political obstacles at home and abroad would not allow us to finish off our opponents, and the North's willingness to sustain huge losses of life over time was already, in the early days of this conflict, turning this into a war of attrition. Ready to commit as many troops and much time as necessary, our enemy held the upper hand. They intended to wait for our resolve to dissolve.[2]

I had arrived at Da Nang one year and two days after the first two battalions of Marines staged an amphibious landing at China Beach and entered Da Nang.

My view of the war changes

Over my twelve months spent in Vietnam, I gradually began to believe this war was not being fought correctly. I even wrote a letter to my dad complaining of the way the war was being waged, but I tore it up instead of mailing it. There were too many restrictions placed on the U.S. military. We dropped a total of 643,000 tons of bombs during the three years of Operation Rolling Thunder,[3] yet American pilots were prohibited, at least in the early days of the war, from attacking strategic targets like MiG air bases in North Vietnam.[4] In South Vietnam, the Viet Cong could strike a blow against a U.S.

---

1   **ARVN** – Army of the Republic of Vietnam, the South Vietnamese army.
2   Wiest, *Essential Histories*, 27-33.
3   Wiest, *Essential Histories*, 27.
4   Rossweti, "Vietnam War."

military position and then retreat across the Cambodian border where our soldiers could not pursue them. Even in-country, military engagement was restricted. A Marine guarding the perimeter of the Da Nang Air Base told me he wasn't allowed to shoot a Viet Cong unless he got permission from his night leader.

Then there was the ammunition shortage. Much of the ordnance dropped by our planes was manufactured in Germany, and at one point during my year in Vietnam, there were not enough German-made bombs to go around. Planes like the F4-C that could have carried multiple bombs under its wings took off with only one under each so the pilots could meet their mission quotas.[5] On the ground, the infantry couldn't get oil for their rifles. It got so bad that parents in the U.S. were shipping oil to their sons in Vietnam.

Toward the end of my tour of duty, the U.S. called a cease-fire to allow diplomats to discuss peace.[6] The net effect was to allow the Viet Cong ample time to bring down the Ho Chi Min Trail more supplies, which they used to attack us once the fighting resumed.

I still believed that the reason for the U.S. military being in Vietnam was honorable—to prevent the Viet Cong and North Vietnam from over-running South Vietnam and spreading Communism throughout that corner of the world. It seemed politics played too large a part in our deployment. The airmen with whom I served felt we should be able to fight with no holds barred—not like we

---

5   Pilots serving in Vietnam had to fly 100 missions. After that they could go home. Some chose to fly two to three missions a day so they could leave Vietnam as early as possible.

6   Rosseti, "Vietnam War."

appeared to be fighting, with our hands tied behind our backs. I, for one, was a firm believer that we would not win this war if we did not make the people backing the Communist insurgents suffer.

For this reason, 29 June 1966 was the proudest day of my entire twelve months in Vietnam. I and the other ground support crewmen at Da Nang Air Base were elated when we were told to put in the air anything that would fly, loaded with bombs and rockets. Planes flew in from Thailand to refuel at the air base, and we knew something big was going on.

Later, our squadron commander Colonel Ottman called us together and showed us movies of what had taken place. As a result of the continued infiltration of Communist guerrillas into South Vietnam, the U.S. had ended a self-imposed moratorium and bombed oil depots around Hanoi and Haiphong, knocking out an estimated 70 percent of the enemy's oil supplies.[7]

That, we all agreed, was how a war should be fought—without pulling punches. For a while, hope ran high that the war was nearing an end. In the long run, though, it didn't have much effect because our planes were still not allowed to touch the Chinese, Russian, German and even Canadian ships that were resupplying North Vietnam. Our political leaders were deathly afraid of triggering a nuclear World War III.[8]

---

7   Rosseti, "Vietnam War."

8   For this reason, they would not approve military actions which had even a slim chance of drawing other super-powers into the conflict.

Living on an air base constantly reminded me of the conflict going on right outside our gates. After a hostile action, our soldiers would bring body bags in from the field. We'd see twenty, thirty, or even forty body bags arranged in neat rows along the flight line, waiting for transport to the States by a C-130 Hercules or a C-141 Starlifter. It rattled me to think there were kids in those bags with mothers, fathers, wives, and children back home. The war seemed to stretch on and on with people being killed like there was no end to the supply.

Our side's devaluation of human life, even those of our enemies, was also unsettling. Cliff described to me one disturbing scene he personally witnessed. Prisoners had been brought to Da Nang via helicopter and were awaiting a C-123 Provider which would transport them to a POW camp. The prisoners sat on the ground in circles of twenty to thirty, facing each other, blindfolded, and hands tied. Two Vietnamese military cops known as CQ guarded each circle of prisoners.

Hauling a compressor to an aircraft parked nearby, Cliff spied a CQ standing behind a prisoner. The prisoner worked to free his hands. "Because he was blindfolded, the prisoner couldn't see the CQ standing behind him," explained my friend. "As soon as he got his hands loose, the prisoner slipped his blindfold up, ran about ten feet and the CQ shot him through the back of the head." Cliff concluded that the CQ had been watching the prisoner untie his hands, just waiting for him to make his move so he (the CQ) would have an excuse to execute him.

BASE SAFETY AN ILLUSION

Living on an airbase protected by mines, wire barriers, and Air Police turned out to be a lot less safe than I had imagined. A couple months before I got to Vietnam, a base cop directing traffic died when the Viet Cong lobbed a mortar over the perimeter where it fell at the cop's feet. My friend Cliff also had a close encounter with a mortar that landed just a few feet from him. Unlike the cop, he lived to tell of it.

Early in our deployment, the Viet Cong tried to over-run Da Nang Air Base, so Command scrambled a Marine fighter loaded with napalm.[9] The fighter would drop its payload as soon as it went airborne, raining fiery death on the attackers. Only one problem— the fighter's front tires were almost flat. Despite incoming mortars, Cliff took the call to deliver an air compressor to the fighter. When he arrived, the crew chief grabbed the air hose, inflated the tires and threw the hose back to Cliff, who immediately steered his tractor off the runway so the fighter could take off.

At that end of the runway, about thirty yards away, stood a guard house, where a Marine carrying an M14 was stationed. "All of a sudden, as I turned my tractor around, I heard an incoming mortar," explained Cliff. "I knew it was close. It hit between the Marine and me and rolled down the runway, but it never exploded." Shak-

---

9   **Napalm** (naphthenic palmitic acid)–an incendiary weapon invented in 1942. It is an extremely flammable, gasoline-based defoliant and antipersonnel weapon that can generate temperatures in excess of 2,000 degrees. "Napalm," *United States History,* http://www.u-s-history.com/pages/h1859.html.

en, Cliff radioed Explosive Ordinance Disposal to deal with the unexploded mortar. As for the Marine, he fainted dead away.

Communist insurgents weren't the only source of danger to base dwellers like us. On 14 May 1966, as Cliff, a couple other airmen, and I walked to work alongside a concrete wall, we heard the popping sound of a machine gun. Looking up, we saw a pattern of bullets spray across the wall two feet above us. We threw ourselves into the nearest bunker but soon realized it was being used to store ammunition. "Let's get out of here," Cliff shouted. "If a mortar comes in, we're done for." Later, we learned the machine gun fire came from fighting between army units loyal to South Vietnamese Prime Minister Nguyen Cao Ky and renegade South Vietnamese marines trying to overthrow the Ky government.[10]

Our own aircraft constituted another danger. During my year in Vietnam, several plane crashes resulted in loss of life. These included a DC-3 *Gooney Bird,* a Marine aircraft that crashed on take-off killing the pilot and eight Marines, and a Navy F-8 Crusader loaded with bombs that lost power on takeoff and crashed into a small hamlet not far from the south end of the runway. The pilot ejected, but the plane went down in the village killing eighty-four people. Then there was the Air Force F-4C that blew both main gear tires on its take-off roll. I heard a POP! POP! that sounded like mortars, but it turned out to be the bombs on the plane. The aircraft

10 Rosseti, "Vietnam War."

sat burning on the runway all night, and every now and then these bombs would explode. Somehow the pilot got out alive.

Despite my growing awareness of our danger, I tried to exude confidence one day in the chow hall when a young airman from New York City asked me, "Are we going to be okay?" I told him, "Yes, we're fine here. We're not in much danger. We're surrounded by the Army and the Marines." He was just a kid and his mother in New York City worried about him. He wanted to reassure her, so I added, "Tell your mother you'll be fine." Personally, I wasn't so sure.

BUILDING THE SOUTH SUB POOL

By the fall of 1966, Cliff Thielman had already taken a job in Control, where plotting boards showed the position of each aircraft and each piece of ground power equipment on the base. Airmen, crowded into this dimly lit hive of activity, spent all their time on the radio, dispatching ground equipment to aircraft. Air conditioned and sandbagged from floor to roof, the Control building ranked as perhaps the safest place on the base.

At one point Cliff tried to get me to join him there. One day, he even brought me inside Control and showed me around. It was impressive; but in the end, I decided that kind of an environment was not for me. For one thing, I didn't like the idea of working inside a dark little building all the time. I liked being outside in the open air, away from all the hustle and bustle. For another, the place was filled with brass—colonels, captains, and majors were all over the place. Cliff wasn't bothered by them, and I had high respect for them, but officers in general made me nervous.

I had begun my tour of duty at the main shop of the 366th FMS located right on the flight line and adjacent to the Marine's ground power shop. Midway through the year, we started constructing a maintenance pool (the sub pool as we called it) at the south end of the base. The sub pool was a mile south of our main shop which was located mid-way along the base's two 10,000 foot runways – one for take-offs and the other for landings.

The 366th FMS tackled major equipment repairs at its main shop, while staff assigned to the south maintenance sub pool performed minor maintenance tasks. The sub pool functioned primarily as a convenient point of storage and dispatch for ground power equipment to aircraft parked at the southern end of the base.

I helped construct the south maintenance sub pool, which we literally built from the ground up. A hundred-square-foot floor formed by laying heavy sheets of perforated, interlocking steel plating served as the main storage space for our inventory of equipment. Each of these four-by-eight-foot sheets weighed 250 to 500 pounds and took four guys to haul. This massive floor saved a lot of grief when monsoon rains turned the rest of the ground into a muddy mess.

We constructed the sub pool on the backside of a revetment—a large concrete U-shaped wall designed to shield two to three aircraft. Besides acting as a shield, revetments were meant to separate aircraft so that, if a mortar came in and hit one aircraft, it wouldn't cause a chain reaction destroying dozens of planes. Walls of the revetment measured ten to twelve feet high and ten to fifteen feet thick. Huge metal heat shields inside each revetment diverted the thrust of the jet engines, allowing pilots to fire up their aircraft without burning up the revetment wall.

The roof of the south maintenance sub pool extended out from the back of the revetment, as a lean-to with four-by-four studs holding it up. We painted the studs with black and yellow diagonal stripes. For the most part, the area under the lean-to was open to the outside. If it was raining, we could pull equipment under this roof to work on it.

We also built a small office at one end of the lean-to, with screen from waist to ceiling and a screened door to keep out mosquitoes. The office contained the seat of an old bus recovered from a salvage yard, a coffee pot purchased at the Marine PX, a desk, and a chair often occupied by Staff Sergeant Jim Beal, who was in charge of the sub pool. Between dispatches, we'd occupy the office and listen to stories of Sergeant Beal's turbulent marriage. Right alongside the office, between our revetment and the next one, ran a JP4 pipeline, carrying jet fuel to the flight line.

FINAL MONTHS AT DA NANG

Christmas Eve 1966 arrived overcast and quiet, courtesy of a two-day truce. Operations at Da Nang Air Base slowed to a trickle, giving everyone an opportunity to think of home. With just over two months to go in my tour of duty, I dared to look into the future.

"Maybe I'll make it back in one piece after all," I thought, as I woofed down a traditional dinner of turkey and dressing at the chow hall and fingered the hand-made record I'd been keeping of the days left in my deployment.

For a while, I had felt that I'd never leave here. The brass had been threatening us, and we'd heard rumors of extending our tour for six additional months. It scared the crap out of us that they might never let us go home. Personally, I didn't think I'd be killed over here, but I felt I might be wounded. That feeling intensified as I watched wounded soldiers loaded on planes bound for hospitals in the Philippines, Japan, or Guam. Often they'd be visible along the flight line on stretchers or standing around a plane with bandaged heads, arms, or legs.

But on Christmas Eve, looking at the days I'd checked off my calendar with the regularity and discipline of the countdown to a Titan rocket launch at Cape Canaveral, I had a little more confidence of heading home soon and in one piece.

Later that evening, I sat in the sub pool office having a beer and shooting the breeze with the other guys unfortunate enough to draw holiday duty. We had nothing to do because of the cease-fire, and it was dark and rainy outside.

All of a sudden, we heard a loud explosion and ran out of the office just in time to watch a giant ball of fire erupt from the ground about a mile south of the runway. "Oh, no!" exclaimed Beal. "Not again!" Flames rose heavenward from the same village the F-8 Crusader had crashed into just a couple months earlier. Beal commandeered a jeep and a set of work lights used for night runway repair, and we headed for the village. We took M16 rifles with us, since Viet Cong were known to be in the area.

As we approached, unhappy residents lined the streets of the little town. At the crash site, we worked to set up our lights. What we witnessed, as we flipped the power switch, was a scene of unbelievable devastation—crushed huts and dead bodies strewn everywhere. We were some of the first to arrive on the scene. The Navy arrived soon after with fire engines and other equipment. But the Marines had the toughest job. They spent the next forty-eight hours collecting burnt bodies and body parts and putting them in bags for identification.[11]

As we later learned, an American Flying Tiger cargo plane inbound from Japan had come down short of our runway and crashed into this unfortunate Vietnamese village just recovering from the earlier disaster. The death toll from this crash reached 125, with forty-two wounded.[12] Counted among the dead were the cargo plane's three-man flight crew and the pilot's wife who came along at the last moment, just to say she'd been in Vietnam.

That shook me up badly. Much of the confidence I had felt earlier in the day faded.

---

11 Jack Moore, untitled Weblog entry posted 9:47 p.m. (Pacific), September 09, 2010, http://www.vwam.com/guestbook/index.php?page=49Cached–Similar (accessed April 13, 2012).

12 "Troubled World Observes Tragedy Marred Yuletide," *The Danville Register* (Danville, VA), Sunday morning, December 25, 1966.

My friend Cliff had similar misgivings. He had been ordered to Vietnam at the same time as me. "When I got my orders, my first thought was—I'm not coming back," he told me. He almost didn't. Besides the unexploded ordnance that landed between him and the Marine guard earlier in the year, Cliff had another close call which he'll tell you about in the next chapter.

1030 HOURS, 26 FEBRUARY 1967

"Almost home," I mouthed without a sound, as I got ready for my night shift at the south maintenance pool. "Almost home," I said again, this time daring to whisper out loud as I buttoned my fatigues and glanced at the "nearly home" ribbon I had pinned to my lapel. Until now, I'd been afraid to say these words with all the bodies and all the near misses my friends and I had experienced; but I was a short-timer now. In seven days I'd be on a plane to San Francisco, and a few days later I'd be discharged from the U.S. Air Force. I hated flying, but my desire to leave Vietnam trumped everything.

I stuffed my discharge orders into my back pocket along with my "countdown" calendar. I even wore my wedding ring, which was a no-no for anyone working with power equipment—but again, I was a short-timer and felt invincible.

It had rained a lot that February, and the U.S. had declared a truce to coincide with Tet, the lunar New Year—a traditional Vietnamese holiday. So there wasn't much work for the ground crews most of that month.

But with diplomatic peace efforts at an impasse, President Johnson had announced the U.S. would resume full-scale bombing of North Vietnam.[13] So with our planes flying cover for the bombers up north, things had gotten pretty busy around the Da Nang Air Base.

"Almost home," I said again under my breath, remembering the military's recent efforts to keep me here. When I went to the base hospital for my discharge physical, the doctor examining me had tried to talk me into staying in the Air Force. Then several of us close to discharge were summoned to a Captain's Call where they urged us to re-enlist. They offered a nice signing bonus and told me I could make staff sergeant if I stayed.

I seriously considered the offer. The last few months I'd had mixed feelings about going home. After my discharge, I'd be without a job and still have the responsibility of supporting a family of four. But I finally decided to take my chances in the civilian world. It would be a struggle for a while, but Judie and I had learned to live on a small income while we were stationed in Duluth. We could do it again.

After deciding not to re-enlist, I began to think about what lay ahead. With my military obligations satisfied, I could go to college on the GI Bill. Or with my experience in electronics, I could easily get a job with Control Data or Honeywell. (Before joining the Air Force, I had submitted an application at Control Data. They said,

13 Rosseti, "Vietnam War."

"Come back when you're done with your military service, and we'll hire you.") I even thought of applying at the Minneapolis-St. Paul International Airport for a job doing basically what I had been doing in Vietnam—working with ground power equipment.

Now I was almost home. With the troop buildup over the last year, we were seeing a lot of fresh faces on base. I thought how lucky I was to have started my tour before all these guys, but then I remembered all the fellows I'd seen go home in the last year that had gotten here before me. I'd keep my fingers crossed and wait my turn. Just a few days left—no, not a few days, but a few hours. I could start counting the hours now. In a little over 200 hours, my plane would leave for California.

At 2200 hours I walked out the gate of Camp Da Nang and caught my last bus to the south maintenance sub pool.

Five hours and ten minutes later, in the early morning hours of 27 February 1967, Viet Cong forces staged an attack on Da Nang Air Base. (See Chapter 1: The Explosion.) The enemy first employed 140 mm unguided rockets during this attack. One rocket landed at the South Maintenance Sub Pool, severely wounding me and killing my twenty-year-old friend and fellow airman Bob Jones.

"All was well with me, but he shattered me; he seized me by the neck and crushed me. He has made me his target."—Job 16:12 (NIV)

CHAPTER 8

The Road to Recovery

TELEGRAM

1016 CST FEB 28 67 MA611

MRS JUDITH C SCHWERMAN, 611 EAST 16ᵀᴴ
ST MPLS

YOUR HUSBAND A1C RONALD L SCHWERMAN
WAS VERY SERIOUSLY INJURED ON 27 FEB 67
IN VIETNAM AS THE RESULT OF A (ROCKET)
ATTACK ON DA NANG AIR BASE BY HOSTILE
FORCES. THE FIRST DIAGNOSIS WAS WOUNDS
MULTIPLE PENETRATING SHRAPNELS IN
ABDOMINAL AREA AND FACE, AND SECOND WAS
TRAUMATIC AMPUTATION BOTH ARMS ABOVE
ELBOW; ALSO AMPUTATION RIGHT LEG BELOW
KNEE. HIS PROGNOSIS IS SERIOUS AND GUARDED
. . . PLEASE ACCEPT MY SINCERE SYMPATHY IN
THIS TIME OF ANXIETY.

LT COL JOSEPH G LUTHER CHIEF, CASUALTY DIVISION DIRECTORATE OF PERSONNEL SERVICES HEADQUARTERS, UNITED STATES AIR FORCE

MARBLE MOUNTAIN

27 FEBRUARY 1967

Despite the finality of the Navy corpsman's assessment, Ron was still alive—but just barely. The truck onto which the corpsman had tossed him transported Ron and others wounded in the rocket attack to a field hospital located five miles south of Da Nang, near the foot of the Marble Mountains. After stabilizing him, the medical staff arranged for Ron's transfer via helicopter to a hospital ship stationed just offshore, in the South China Sea where greater attention could be given to his life-threatening injuries.

Fading in and out of consciousness, Ron remembers only a few images and conversations with medical personnel and visitors during his final four days in Vietnam.

Hours, or more likely days, after being tossed onto a truck bed at Da Nang, I awoke and saw my squadron commander standing over me.

As Colonel Ottman had walked through our newly constructed barracks every Friday for inspection, I often wondered if he knew we were in the middle of fighting a war. *"A squadron commander must have better things to do,"* I thought then. But now, I felt honored he had taken the time to visit one of his wounded men.

"Do you know the extent of your wounds?" asked Colonel Ottman. I moved my head in a gesture of affirmation. One of the hospital corpsmen had informed me that I had lost both arms and my right leg below the knee, and that my left leg was badly damaged. I asked Colonel Ottman about the others at the sub pool. He told me A1C Bob Jones had died in the same explosion that had wounded me. Two other crewmembers had sustained lesser injuries and would be okay. We talked a little more, and then I passed out.

Later, the colonel phoned to inform me that an Air Force policeman with a machine gun had been stationed in a bunker 150 feet east of the sub pool and had witnessed the explosion. Despite the fact that I was surrounded by fire (the explosion had punctured the JP4 line, spraying jet fuel all over) and with more rockets incoming, this policeman got out of his bunker and ran to where I lay. From my already torn fatigues, he fashioned tourniquets which he applied between my limbs and my body, to stop the blood flow. That action very likely saved my life. The U.S. Air Force later awarded that policeman a medal for heroism.

I woke again to the gentle prodding of a young Navy corpsman. "General Walt is here to see you," he whispered. Stationed at Da Nang, Marine General Lewis Walt commanded all American military units in the northern sector of Vietnam. Now, the leader of the Infantry Combat Regiment had come to see me. I do not recall much of our conversation, but I do remember that he laid a Purple

Heart on my chest. *"I must be in bad shape,"* I reasoned, *"if a general wants to give me the Purple Heart before I die."* I closed my eyes and dozed off again.

My friend Cliff Thielman also visited me. The medical personnel had me well-sedated, and I don't recall much of our conversation, so I'm relying on his account of the story:

> **Cliff:** *"I was working in the Control building early the morning of February 27. It was still dark when we heard the incoming rockets. Despite Control's sandbagged walls, we all scrambled out the door and ran for a bunker about twenty yards away. There were six to eight of us, and I was the third or fourth man out the door. Before reaching the bunker, a rocket exploded immediately in back of us. The guy running just behind me took shrapnel in his back and died instantly. If it hadn't been for him, I might not be here today.*
>
> *"About an hour after the attack, Sergeant Doyle came into the control room and told me you had been injured. I turned to the colonel and said, 'Sir, I need to leave. My buddy, Ron, has been hurt bad, and I want to see if he's all right.' He handed me the keys to his jeep, and I drove to the field hospital.*
>
> *"When I walked into your tent, you were talking pretty normal, but it was obvious you were pumped up on morphine. The longer I stood there looking at your wounds the more sick to my stomach I became. I'd never seen a*

person I cared for in this kind of situation. I could feel myself choking up just talking to you, so I made up some excuse about going out to check the jeep. On the way out, I met another sergeant from our squadron coming in to see you. 'How's Ron?' he asked. 'Not good,' I said, shaking my head. Then, I sat down on the ground and bawled."[1]

On 3 March 1967, four days after the Monday morning rocket attack, I woke as corpsmen prepared me for my journey back to the U.S. They transferred me to a stretcher and carried me aboard a waiting helicopter, its rotors already turning, for a short return trip to Da Nang Air Base. Throughout the flight, a Marine with an M-60 machine gun sat in the open doorway. He looked over at me as if to attract my attention. Then he fired a few rounds into the rice paddies below. Looking back at me, he smiled as if to say, "Maybe I can get some revenge for you." It's one of my parting recollections of Vietnam. Everybody was angry.

As we approached Da Nang Air Base, I lost consciousness again. I woke up as the corpsmen carried me aboard a C-130 Hercules,[2] and I saw female nurses for the first time in my deployment. The aircraft taxied along the same runway I had walked or ridden over so many times during the past year. I strained to look out a little round window and saw an Air Force policeman standing there with his dog. *"This is the*

---

1   Cliff Thielman, phone interview, June 18, 2011.
2   The C-130 Hercules, built by Lockheed, was a four-engine turboprop used in the Vietnam War for troop transport and medical evacuation.

last time I will travel this strip and in a few seconds I will leave Vietnam forever," I thought. *"The war is over for me now...."* How wrong I was.

I lost consciousness again as the plane left the ground and climbed to cruising altitude.

TELEGRAM

153A CST MAR 3 67 MA034

MRS JUDITH C SCHWERMAN, 611 EAST 16TH ST MPLS

. . . YOUR HUSBAND, A1C RONALD SCHWERMAN . . . (HAS BEEN) AIR EVACUATED TO THE USAF HOSPITAL, CLARK AIR BASE, PHILIPPINES.

LT COL JOSEPH G LUTHER CHIEF, CASUALTY DIVISION DIRECTORATE OF PERSONNEL SERVICES HEADQUARTERS, UNITED STATES AIR FORCE

USAF HOSPITAL
CLARK AIR BASE, PHILIPPINES

2 MARCH 1967

Oblivious of time passing, I woke again in the hospital at Clark Air Base.

On my arrival in the Philippines, my wife and my parents received telegrams informing them that my injuries no longer seriously endangered my life and that I would soon be air evacuated to the U.S. Within hours, however, another telegraph arrived stating that I had contracted pneumonia. The Air Force listed me as "very seriously ill" and stated that my prognosis was "guarded." The pneumonia complicated the tracheostomy[3] performed as they stabilized me in Vietnam and forced a delay in my return to the mainland.

I have little memory of my eleven-day stay in the Philippines, except that I shared a room with two wounded Marines. The Marine on my left had lost a leg below the knee.[4] Screaming and crying a lot, he obviously had a hard time accepting his injury. Examining the stump where the man's leg used to be, his doctor looked over at me and said to the Marine, "You think you got it bad, look at that guy." I thought, *"Thanks a lot."* Maybe the doc thought I was still unconscious.

On my right, a Marine spoke by phone to his father in Michigan. The medical staff had enclosed this serviceman's head in some sort of wire cage with ropes and weights running in all directions. I heard him say, "Hi, Dad. It's Mike." Tears began rolling down this young man's face, and he began to quiver as he told how he had been point man on a patrol ambushed by the Viet Cong. He had been shot in the neck. "The doctors say I'm going to be okay, Dad," said the

---

3 Done to bypass obstructions in the upper airway, a tracheostomy is a surgically created opening in the neck leading directly to the trachea (the breathing tube). "Tracheostomy," *MedicineNet.com,* http://www.medicinenet.com/tracheostomy/article.htm (accessed April 27, 2012)

4 Over 10,000 American soldiers lost at least one limb in Vietnam. "Vietnam as Statistics" http://home.earthlink.net/~aircommando1/Vietnam.htm (accessed Jan. 8, 2013)

Marine, struggling for control over his emotions. "I might be back in the States soon," he said, adding, "I'll call you when I get back."

Tears formed in the corners of my eyes, as I thought how hurt this father must be to know his son was badly wounded and that he could not be at his son's bedside. All at once I felt very warm and comfortable, and I returned to a welcome drug-induced sleep.

As for my own lost limbs and my prospects for the future, I do not recall feeling any particular emotion—not like the two Marines. I wasn't really scared, and I had yet to consider how the loss of my arms and leg would affect me. I was still struggling to survive.

Besides feeling for my roommate's father, the only emotion I recall showing was anger directed against an NCO posted in my room. At Clark Air Base they assigned someone to watch me at all times. I asked this man for a drink of water and he replied, "No, I can't give you anything." At that, I flew into a rage and swore at him, even though he outranked me. Truth was, I wasn't supposed to drink or eat anything. My spleen and diaphragm had been hit by shrapnel, my liver had been injured, and my intestines were all torn up. But at that particular moment, I didn't want to be bothered by the facts. I was very thirsty.

Mercifully, I was unconscious most of the time.

While I was hospitalized at Clark, a Continental airliner carrying my friend Cliff Thielman back to the States stopped briefly in the Philippines. Cliff tried to get off the plane to see me, but was denied permission. His plane soon took off for Guam and then for San Francisco.

I did not know that my status was being broadcast daily on the public address system at Da Nang Air Base and followed closely by my squadron. In his pockets, Cliff carried hundreds of dollars raised by the men of the 366th FMS for me and my family. "Most of us gave our whole paychecks," Cliff later told me. Following his 8 March discharge from the Air Force, Cliff boarded a commercial flight from San Francisco to Minneapolis. He did not tell Judie he was coming, and by his own account did not tell her the severity of my condition. Prior to leaving Vietnam, Cliff had called the hospital, and based on the information he was given, had concluded that I was not expected to live.

Arriving in Minneapolis, he located Judie and presented her with the gift of money. "I tried to give her some hope of what the future would be like," said Cliff, "but I didn't paint as bad a picture as I believed it to be—I just couldn't."

For the next several days, it appeared that Cliff's worse fears would be realized. Despite the best efforts of the medical personnel at Clark Air Force Base, the infection inside me continued to rage. Finally the doctors decided to air evacuate me to the United States—specifically to Wilford Hall, a 1000-bed hospital at Lackland Air Force Base near San Antonio, Texas.

They packed me up and put me aboard a bus which delivered me to a C-141 Starlifter, a big military transport parked along the runway at Clark. I remember someone was at the front of the bus giving instructions on what to do if the plane went down in the water. I asked them, "What do I do if the plane goes down?" He chuckled and said, "We'll take care of you . . ." which may have meant, "you'd be dead—you wouldn't have a chance." The fact that I remember that exchange tells me that, to some extent, I was aware of my situation.

The hospital personnel loaded me aboard the Starlifter. I recall an Air Force nurse, a tall Puerto Rican woman with very dark hair, who was helping the wounded get settled on the aircraft. Some of them could walk on board, at least with the aid of crutches, and others like me were carried aboard on gurneys.

Whether it was real or a dream, I do not know. But in my memory the tall Puerto Rican nurse gave me a milkshake to drink. I suppose it was a dream as I was NPO,[5] but in my mind it represented an act of sustenance.

TELEGRAM

1117A CST MAR 14 67 MC129

MRS JUDITH C SCHWERMAN, 611 EAST 16ᵀᴴ ST MPLS

. . . A REPORT JUST RECEIVED STATES THAT (YOUR HUSBAND'S) CONDITION IS NOT GOOD. HE HAS BEEN AIR EVACUATED TO WILFORD HALL USAF HOSPITAL, LACKLAND AIR FORCE BASE TEXAS . . .

LT COL JOSEPH G LUTHER CHIEF, CASUALTY DIVISION DIRECTORATE OF PERSONNEL SERVICES HEADQUARTERS, UNITED STATES AIR FORCE

---

5   **NPO** – Latin for "nothing by mouth." Medical acronym indicating to medical personnel that no food or beverage may be consumed by the patient.

US NAVAL HOSPITAL
GUAM

But air evacuation to the U.S. on that day did not happen. Soon after we lifted off from Clark Air Base, I became violently ill, and my temperature spiked at 107.9 degrees, forcing the pilot to land our plane at Anderson Air Force Base in Guam. A fairly high-ranking doctor, a bird colonel, came aboard to assess my condition. "Get him off the plane," he ordered. "He's staying here."

As crew members prepared to take me off the Starlifter, I distinctly remember that Puerto Rican nurse coming up to my stretcher, leaning over and speaking to me. "I'll be back to get you," she said. "Don't forget that . . . I'll be back to get you," she repeated.

They took me to a large naval hospital located on Guam where the severity of my illness and side-affects of the drugs used to keep me alive further blurred the lines between hallucination and reality.

Reality: I had developed double-lobar pneumonia and had infection all over my body. My attending physician gave it to me straight. "I don't know if we can keep you alive, Ron," he said. "I'll give you fifty-fifty odds. We're going to try some medication and hopefully you'll survive, but you may not." For some reason, that didn't scare me. Maybe I was too high on morphine to care.

Hallucination: During my first hours in the hospital, I had the weird sense that I was in an officer's club. Everyone else was up at the bar having drinks, talking and partying, while I lay on this gurney. That was probably the morphine.

Reality: To get my body temperature down, they put me in a bath of alcohol and ice cubes. I felt awful due to my fever, but that bath was truly terrible to endure.

Hallucination: I dreamed that the screws on my bed turned into big faucets where I could get Coke or Pepsi. I was so thirsty.

My prognosis was, in fact, so grave that the Air Force contacted Judie two days after I arrived at the naval hospital, offering to fly her to my side. The American Red Cross donated $300 toward her travel expense to Travis Air Force Base where she boarded a plane for Guam.

TELEGRAM

918P CST MAR 16 67 MB565

MRS JUDITH C SCHWERMAN, 611 EAST 16TH ST MPLS

. . . THE ATTENDING PHYSICIAN STATES THAT YOUR PRESENCE AT (YOUR HUSBAND'S) BEDSIDE IS ADVISABLE FROM A MEDICAL STANDPOINT . . . REPORT AS SOON AS POSSIBLE TO THE OVERSEAS PASSENGER TERMINAL AT TRAVIS AIR FORCE BASE, FAIRFIELD, CALIFORNIA, FOR AIR TRANSPORTATION WHICH HAS BEEN SCHEDULED FOR YOU . . . .

LT COL JOSEPH G LUTHER CHIEF, CASUALTY DIVISION DIRECTORATE OF PERSONNEL SERVICES HEADQUARTERS, UNITED STATES AIR FORCE

Judie came and stayed at my bedside for the rest my time in Guam. I did not die. Ever-so-slowly, I improved. Between hallucinations, my reality grew more hopeful.

Hallucination: I imagined that people would come into my hospital room and dump garbage containing needles on my bed. I would say to Judie, "Get somebody to take this garbage out of here." Judie would shake her head, "There's nothing on the bed, Ron."

Reality: I would cough and phlegm would shoot out of my tracheostomy tube, hitting the ceiling of my hospital room. That was not a dream. When I finally left that room, the ceiling was so phlegm-covered it had to be repainted. Though disgusting to consider, it hinted at my steady recovery.

Hallucination: I dreamed of being out on Lake Superior at twenty degrees-below-zero and the lake was frozen over. I could see water underneath the ice, and I was dying of thirst. So I tried to get through the ice to get a drink.

Reality: Someone stuck a straw through ice, and I was actually sucking water. I thought this was part of my dream, but it was real. A nurse was giving me my first liquid by mouth in many days.

Western Union Telegrams sent by the Air Force every four to five days to my parents in Minneapolis gradually reported my prognosis changing from "not good" to "guarded" to "satisfactory" as the medical staff got the infection under control. Eventually, after removing some shrapnel from my intestines, they offered me a little solid food. I had become so thin, and they wanted me to gain some weight. They asked if I liked beer, and I said "yes," so they brought me a bottle. I took one sip and it tasted awful—like drinking formaldehyde. But I was eating.

They dressed my wounds every few hours, including changing the wrappings on what remained of my right leg. Judie walked in one day when they had me unwrapped. She was shocked to see the bone sticking out of the stump by several inches. Having my wounds dressed was extremely painful, but I credit the naval hospital on Guam for saving my life.

Early in my stay there, President Lyndon Johnson flew to the island for a meeting with South Vietnamese Premier Nguyen Cao Ky. Covering this March event, *Newsweek* magazine reported, "Before leaving (Guam) the President made an unpublicized visit to (the) U.S. Naval Hospital, where he paid a call on wounded American servicemen from Vietnam. One was a triple amputee—with only his left leg intact—whose wife was at his bedside." [6] That was Judie and me.

Newsweek reported that Judie asked the President, "Aren't you proud of him?" and that Mr. Johnson "could not speak," but "gripped her hand and moved on." According to *Newsweek,* the President later confided to an aide, "I haven't slept very well since."[7]

I do recall the president standing over my bed. He was a big man, and contrary to the magazine story, I recall him asking, "How are you feeling, son?" Judie put her hand over my tracheostomy tube, permitting me to speak. "I'm doing okay," I said to the president, but I don't remember much after that. I guess I lost consciousness.

---

6   "A Trip to Guam – and a No from Ho," *Newsweek*, 3 April 1967, 27.
7   "A Trip to Guam," *Newsweek*, 27.

A day or so after the President's visit, a doctor stopped by my room. "Who are you?" he demanded. Apparently, the White House had just called to inquire about me, and this doctor thought I must be some kind of war hero or politician—or both. From that day on, both the White House and my squadron at Da Nang Air Base received regular updates on my condition.

Vietnam still figured in my thinking, both waking and sleeping. Two Navy pilots in the room next to me had been shot up in Vietnam. While recovering from their wounds, they peeked in every so often to say hi, and day or night I could hear B-52's taking off from Anderson Air Force Base, headed to Vietnam to drop their payload.

One other change I recall as I recovered was my increased interest in the spiritual side of life. I asked to talk with a pastor, and a Navy chaplain came to see me. After his initial visit, he came regularly and gave me communion.

At first, I wasn't allowed to drink anything, so the chaplain would dip the bread in the wine and touch my lips. I hadn't taken communion my entire year in Vietnam, but now it became very important to me. I wanted assurance that my sins were forgiven in case I would die. Perhaps this stemmed from my earlier years when I feared going to hell for not believing in Jesus. Though I had professed belief, my life certainly did not reflect my faith and trust in him. But at least I was thinking about God, which was something I had not done for years.

After seven weeks, I had recovered enough for the Air Force to complete my evacuation to Texas. A Navy doctor accompanied Judie and me during the entire flight to San Antonio.

I remember the night being dark and the weather being warm and tropical when the hospital staff took me outside to a waiting C-141 Starlifter. "As they were loading me on the plane, the same tall Puerto Rican nurse came up to my gurney. She smiled and declared, "I told you I'd come back to get you, and here I am."

CHAPTER 9

Further Down the Road

Wilford Hall, Lackland Air Force Base
San Antonio, Texas

18 April 1967

I do not remember the flight from Guam to Texas, except for the landing. We hit the runway hard. I confess to thinking some unkind thoughts about the pilot. Then, with the plane parked and airstairs in place, the crew refused to allow anyone off the C-141 Starlifter.

Our impatience turned to extreme curiosity as an official-looking black car approached the plane and stopped at the base of the stairs. A dark-suited gentleman emerged, climbed the steps, and entered the airplane. He asked for me. A nurse led him back to where I lay on my gurney.

The man produced an envelope bearing the White House seal and declared, "President Johnson welcomes you back to the United States of America." He opened the envelope, unfolded the enclosed letter, and began to read:

THE WHITE HOUSE
WASHINGTON

April 18, 1967

Dear Airman Schwerman:

I want to be among the first to welcome you home and wish you well.

Your road has been long and your battle hard—but now that you have come this far, the remainder of life's journey must surely be more hopeful.

I know that you and your wife will face the future with courage and confidence. You will have my pride and my prayers accompanying you every mile of the way.

God bless you both.

Sincerely,

Lyndon Johnson

The president's spokesman handed the letter to Judie and retraced his steps to the waiting car, after which everyone was free to deplane.

An ambulance transported me from the airport, on the north side of San Antonio, to Wilford Hall, a 1,000-bed hospital southwest of the city. The hospital was located on the grounds of Lackland Air Force Base, where I had begun my basic training four years to the day earlier.[1] Planes brought patients daily from all over the world to this premier medical facility. Arriving at Wilford Hall, I met the physician who would work tirelessly—and ruthlessly make *me* work—over the next seven months to put me back together. A major in the U.S. Air Force, Dr. Michael S. Gurvey stopped at my room as I was getting settled. After introducing himself, he asked, "Is there anything I can get you?" I asked for a cigarette.

"You haven't smoked for weeks—why don't you quit?" suggested the physician. I declined. Ironically, Dr. Gurvey smoked, too. As we became better acquainted, he would come into my room, pull up a chair, smoke a cigarette and shoot the bull.

In his official capacity, however, Dr. Gurvey was an excellent surgeon and all business. He would operate on me many times during my stay in Texas. I had already come through several emergency surgeries at Clark AFB and on Guam, just to get me back to the U.S. Now that they were getting my infection under control, the team of surgeons at Wilford Hall could take their time and make

---

1   I even pulled one day of KP at Wilford Hall while I was in boot camp.

revisions to those earlier operations. They trimmed my protruding bones and pulled my skin over the ends to form stumps for future prosthetics. They removed shrapnel and several teeth lodged in my sinuses, and they reconstructed my broken jaw.

To heal the jaw, they wired it shut, and everything I ate had to go through a grinder. Wire cutters and a rubber tube were taped to the wall near my bed. If I started choking, the nursing staff could use the wire cutters to free my jaw. If I started bleeding, they'd use the rubber tube as a tourniquet to stop the flow.

This way of taking in food got old really fast. Once, the kitchen staff brought chicken that had been ground into a malt-like beverage. They expected me to drink it. "Take this back and bring me back some real chicken," I roared. With my health improving, I craved solid food and found the energy to campaign for it.

My first few weeks in Texas, the staff kept me in a circle bed which they turned every couple of hours to prevent bed sores.[2] They put a blue pad on the floor to catch the spit and blood dripping from my mouth while I was on my stomach.

Since I had had pneumonia, the staff gave me medicated breathing treatments every four hours to heal my lungs. They put a green tube in my mouth and told me to breathe deeply. I hated that thing. It hurt to inhale.

---

2 **Circle Bed** – a bed mounted between two circular bars. Powered by an electric motor, the bed is able to be rotated 180 degrees so that the patient is either on his back or on his stomach.

Judie flew with me from Guam to Texas and continued to visit me daily. Early in my stay at Wilford Hall, my mother and father also flew to Texas, accompanied by my older daughter. Pam seemed to adapt easily to my injuries, to the point where she stood calmly at my bedside holding a cigarette to my lips when I wanted a smoke.

My father, too, seemed to take my injuries in stride. My mother, on the other hand, took them hard. One day during a family visit, two corpsmen came to get me for my daily whirlpool bath. They took me down the hall to a big metal bathtub shaped like a figure eight. They placed me on a stretcher suspended by chains and lowered me into the bath. Next, they added medication to the bath water and turned on the jets. That daily half-hour whirlpool bath helped my wounds heal. But on this particular day my left knee bent as they transferred me. It hurt terribly, and I screamed. Back in my room, I saw tears in my mother's eyes. She had heard me scream and had been crying.

My family soon left, and after a while Judie left, too. When her grandmother died, she traveled back to Minnesota for the funeral and stayed there. It was the right thing to do, of course. She had already been gone for over a month, and our daughters needed her there. Angry and depressed, I needed her too but was too proud to say it. When she called, she asked me if I wanted her to come back down, "No," I said stubbornly. "Just stay up there." I still wasn't good at expressing my feelings.

Two nurses tried to boost my spirits. A nice looking woman by the name of Lieutenant Graffelman would come to my room in the evenings just to talk and keep me company. She and another nurse, Lieutenant McDermott, would constantly argue over who was going to feed me. But when I needed a bedpan, they were nowhere in sight. It was always a corpsman who took care of those less pleasant duties.

When I first arrived at Wilford Hall, I met another nurse who helped me adjust during the first few weeks. Her name was Elaine Carlson. I'll let Elaine, the evening shift supervisor at this world-renown medical center, tell her story of those weeks.

> **Elaine:** *"One day, we received notice a triple amputee was coming direct from Saigon . . . we reserved a private room for him because we knew he was badly infected and would have to be kept in isolation. So, we put him on the seventh floor, and as supervisor I visited Ron every evening I worked . . .*
>
> *"I remember thinking how very depressing it must be for this man, in his twenties, to be alone in isolation, having lost both arms and a leg. I was afraid Ron might try suicide, although I could imagine no way he could accomplish it. He couldn't save up his pills because he didn't have a hand to hold them. He couldn't stab himself with a knife and he couldn't even throw himself out of a seventh floor window because he couldn't walk.*
>
> *"Eventually the infection improved, and we were able to transfer Ron to a five-bed ward. I was glad for the move, thinking it would help him to be with the other airmen.*

"Then one night while I was making rounds, a corpsman approached and told me, 'Airman Schwerman[3] is better.' He explained that a boot with an infection in his hand had been admitted to Ron's ward.[4] The attending nurse mixed a solution of soap and medication in hot water and told the young airman to soak his hand for one-half hour every four hours. After the nurse left, Ron called the boot over to his bed. 'What are you here for?' asked the triple-amputee. When the boot told about his infection, Ron shook his head sadly. Holding up the stump of his right arm, he exclaimed, 'That's the way it started with me and look what happened.'

"The young airman turned white as a ghost and began to shake, until Ron started laughing and informed him, 'I'm only kidding.'

"The corpsman said he knew Sergeant Schwerman was out of danger because he could joke with the wide-eyed young man about his missing limbs. From then on, we forgot our sympathy for Ron and just thoroughly enjoyed him."[5]

I did benefit from being moved to a ward. In isolation, all I could do was watch TV. In the ward, I became friends with the other patients, and we had some good times together. We would

---

3   During Ron's stay in Texas, the U.S. Air Force changed all their designations for rank. Ron entered Wilford Hall as an Airman First Class, but he left Wilford Hall seven months later as a Sergeant.

4   **Boot** – an Airman Basic; first level airman, fresh from boot camp.

5   Elaine Carlson, personal interview, April 23, 2011.

tell jokes and stories, they would hold cigarettes for me, and a B-52 pilot who was ambulatory always asked if I wanted anything from the vending machines downstairs. My outlook improved, and with it my physical health.

As I felt better, I started asking about some questions that had not occurred to me in the weeks before, when I was struggling to stay alive. I wondered, "What did they do with my amputated arms?" Someone told me that my arms and right leg had been flown back to the U.S. and were stored, for legal purposes, in a building near the medical center. After that, said my informant, they'd be cremated. I was also told some people actually hold funerals for their limbs. I'm not sure how much of that was true.

Another question has bugged me ever since. "Whatever happened to my wedding band?" Judie received my watch along with my other belongings from Vietnam, but my wedding band was never located.

Within a month after my arrival at Wilford Hall, my squadron commander Colonel Ottman sent a letter to Judie along with a check in the amount of $4000. "This amount," he said, "is a joint contribution by all members of the squadron in hopes that in some way it might ease certain burdens that you and Ron have acquired as a result of his injuries." The letter went on to explain that the contributions were made at a squadron party held in my honor. The Colonel even enclosed some photos taken at the party.

GETTING BACK ON THE ROAD

My recovery at Wilford Hall involved more than eliminating infection and undergoing reconstructive surgery. I had to strengthen and tone muscles which lay unused on gurneys or hospital beds for almost two months. At first, a female therapist would come to my room daily and work with the stumps of my arms. She reminded me of an Amazon—tall and muscular. She held my stumps while she worked the muscles, and it hurt a lot. They didn't bend the way they were supposed to.

Learning to get around on my own also proved difficult. One day, two nurses came into my room and announced, "We're going to get you up in a wheelchair today." Over my protestations, they put me in the chair, but I couldn't sit up. My back didn't bend, so I effectively had to lay in the wheelchair. I kept sliding down and calling out, "Pull me up! I'm falling out of the chair!" It took almost a week to train those dormant muscles to stretch and bend again. Finally I could be in a wheelchair for an extended period of time without falling over.

Despite the medical team's best efforts, not everything worked. In preparation for the prosthetic devices that would one day function as my arms and hands, Dr. Gurvey performed several "revisionary" surgeries. One of those surgeries involved taking a skin graft from the outside of my upper thigh and attaching it to the end of my left arm stump. He did this rather than cut off additional bone to get enough arm skin to pull over the end of the stump.

The more bone that is left, he explained, the better the prosthesis would fit.

A short time after the surgery a corpsman took me for a whirlpool bath. A half-hour later, as he brought me up out of the tub, the whole apparatus jerked and fell a couple of inches. I swung the stump of my left arm to catch myself and hit one of the chains suspending my stretcher. That action tore the recently grafted skin right off.

The corpsman called Dr. Gurvey to come and examine the damage. He was furious—not at anybody in particular, just that the graph had not worked. In the end, he cut off a little more bone and sewed it up again.

Dr. Gurvey also tried to rehabilitate my left leg, which had been injured but not detached in the rocket explosion. The shrapnel had entered my lower leg, sparing the femur but breaking my tibia and fibula. My left knee also gave me excruciating pain when bent, though it bent normally under anesthesia. Giving up on the knee, the surgeon eventually decided to cast my left leg to allow the broken bones to fuse together.

The cast ran from my thigh down to my ankle. It itched terribly, so I had someone shove a stick down the cast and scratch the spot that itched. When he pulled the stick out, it was covered with blood. Dr. Gurvey took me down to the casting room where he cut a window in the cast and found a hunk of shrapnel sticking out of my leg. It had worked its way to the surface and become infected. To limit the risk to other patients, Dr. Gurvey put me in isolation again.

I had had enough of isolation, so I decided to rebel. The very next day, when two corpsmen came with a gurney to take me down to physical therapy, I refused. "No, I'm not going," I told them. "I'm in isolation. How can I go down to PT?" My protest went on for a couple of days. Finally, Dr. Gurvey came to my room and asked me what was wrong. I told him that I wouldn't go down there. "Yes you will!" said the major-physician firmly. "May I remind you that you're still in the Air Force and you are to obey orders." I took that statement seriously and ended my little revolt.

Soon after, Dr. Gurvey allowed another patient named John to room with me. John served as a corpsman on this ward. He had contracted an infection, so they stuck him in isolation with me. He would take care of me and provide some company, they reasoned. We became good friends, and one day, we got the bright idea that we would play a joke on Lieutenant Graffelman. I got on the intercom and called out, "Nurse Graffelman! I'm bleeding." She came running into my room and found us chuckling. It was funny to us, but it wasn't funny to her, and she was mad. She gave me an official Air Force ass chewing and let me know very bluntly that wasn't something to joke about.

During my time in Texas, I got to know a number of interesting people. In addition to the B-52 pilot of whom I spoke, a four-star general came up to me while I waited for an X-ray and started a conversation with me. As this General Lawrence and I talked, I remember thinking, *"That's a whole lot of stars on your shoulders, and you're just shooting the breeze with me, like we were buddies."* Another time Al Capp, the illustrator who drew the Steve Canyon comic strip, came up to my room. He drew a girl dressed like one of the characters in his cartoon and gave the drawing to me.

I also became friends with a C-130 pilot who would come to my ward and play chess with me. He was a good player and would get a little irritated if I'd put him in check. I remember him saying that he couldn't fly anymore because he had lost a thumb he need-ed for the trim controls.

What these encounters and friendships taught me, I guess, is that all these pilots and brass who had intimidated me in the past were a lot like me.

THE ROAD AHEAD

After each surgical revision, physical therapists would work with me. One therapist strapped a pylon[6] to the stump of my left leg to get me used to what it would be like to wear prosthesis. He had me walking between parallel bars. When I got to the end, he made me turn around by myself and come back. I was scared to death, but he was a pusher—he should have been a Marine!

Soon afterwards, the Air Force sent someone to talk with me about prosthetic limbs. He was an African-American who had lost

---

6   **Pylon** – an artificial lower limb, often a narrow vertical support consisting of a socket with wooden side supports and rubber-clad peg limb. "The Free Dictionary by Farlex" http://medical-dictionary.thefreedictionary.com/pylon

one arm and two legs—and he was walking with prostheses. I remember him speaking positively about artificial limbs and what you could do with them. He gave me hope that I would be able to do quite a bit more than I could do at the present time. I even lay awake at night in my hospital bed, moving my limbs as if I was practicing walking.

What I would do for a job, I did not know. I had no concrete ideas about how I would survive or support my family. Any ideas about what the future would be like came from what the people working with me told me about prosthetic limbs. These were mostly generalities. I wondered whether I would ever be able to use a screw driver, a soldering iron or other tools familiar to me before the attack. I imagined myself in a desk job, perhaps working for the government. That might be the only organization willing to employ a person with my disabilities.

All I knew for sure was that after six months at Big Willy (as the long-time residents called Wilford Hall Medical Center) I was close to going home to Minneapolis. Once my infection healed, Dr. Gurvey told me I would be as healthy as anybody. The only medical challenges I faced were being fitted with prostheses and some work needed on my teeth. I could address those issues at the Veterans Administration Medical Center in Minneapolis. I wanted to go home. My wife and kids were in Minneapolis, and I hadn't been there in a long time.

I could have gone home sooner, but I hadn't earned enough credits to qualify for disability assistance under the Social Security

Administration. Someone in the business office at the Texas hospital realized this and came up to my room one day. "We're going to keep you in Texas, on the Air Force payroll, for a month or two longer," they told me, "just long enough for you to earn the full twenty credits you need." They did, and then they sent me home. I've been grateful for their thoughtfulness ever since.

On 24 October 1967, after more than seven months at Big Willy, I was discharged to the VA Hospital in Minneapolis.

Top left, Ron Schwerman at seven years and seven months; *top right*, Ron and his mother, Evelyn Schwerman, on his high school graduation day; *below that*, Ron in his U.S. Air Force dress blues; *bottom*, Ron's Aerospace Ground Equipment class at Chanute Air Force Base in Rantoul, Illinois. Ron is in the front row, third from the right.

Top left, LeRoy Knudson, half-brother, pins the groom's flower before Ron's 1964 wedding; *top right,* Ron holds his daughter Pam; *center,* F-4C fighters parked in revetment at Da Nang Air Base, Vietnam; *below that,* Ron with compressor used to service aircraft.

Top, Ron poses between two bombs and the fuel tank of an F-4C fighter; *bottom left*, fellow airman Cliff Thielman in front of Ron's tent at Da Nang Air Base; *bottom right*, a Vietnamese mama-san who provided housekeeping for Ron's lodging at Camp Da Nang

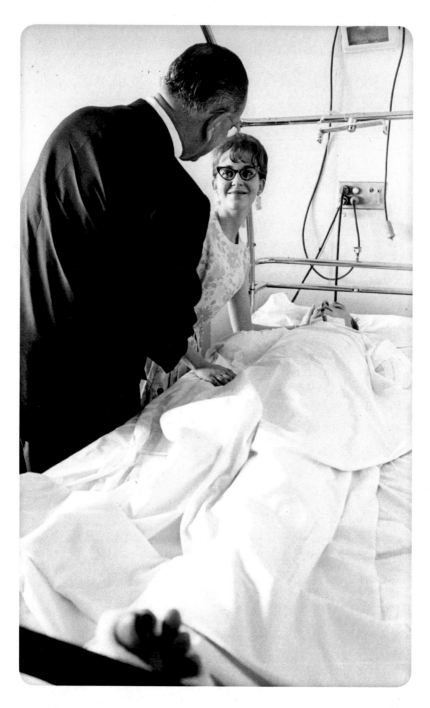

President Lyndon B. Johnson meeting Judie and Ron Schwerman at the U.S. Naval Hospital in Guam.

THE WHITE HOUSE
WASHINGTON

April 18, 1967

Dear Airman Schwerman:

I wanted to be among the first to welcome you
home and wish you well.

Your road has been long and your battle hard --
but now that you have come this far, the remainder
of life's journey must surely be more hopeful.

I know that you and your wife will face the future
with courage and confidence. You will have my
pride and my prayers accompanying you every
mile of the way.

God bless you both.

Sincerely,

A/1C Ronald Schwerman, AF 17649924
Wilfred Hall Hospital
Lackland Air Force Base

AUSTIN, TEXAS

Dear Mr. and Mrs. Schwerman:

Your real estate agent, Harry Jensen, has written
me that you are moving into your new home later
this month. I was delighted to learn that you are
doing so well. But, having had the opportunity to
meet both of you in Guam and to feel your courageous
spirit, I expected it.

I hope the years ahead bring every happiness to you
and your family.

Sincerely,

Mr. and Mrs. Ronald Schwerman
9533 Chicago Avenue
South Bloomington, Minnesota 55421

July 14, 1969

Top, a letter from President Lyndon B. Johnson welcoming Ron back to the U.S. The letter was personally read by a presidential aide to Ron, aboard his air evacuation flight from Guam to Texas; *below that*, a letter from the former president who continued to track Ron's recovery for months and years after meeting him in Guam

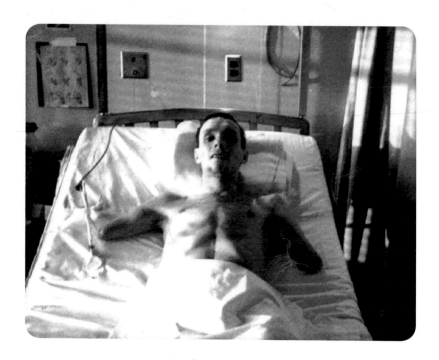

Top, Ron Schwerman in his hospital bed at Wilford Hall, Lackland Air Force Base, Texas; *bottom left*, Ron's NCOIC Sergeant Meyers collects contributions for the Schwerman's at a fundraiser held on the Da Nang Air Base in the weeks following Ron's injury; *bottom right*, Ron walks with help of a peg strapped to stump of his leg during rehab at Wilford Hall in Texas. (Photo Credit: Captain Robert L. Arledge, USAF, BSC)

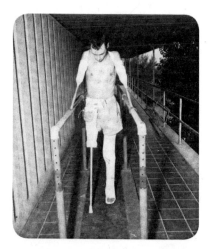

Top, daughter Rhonda (Schwerman) Zielske, Ron Schwerman, and Pam (Schwerman) Yanish; bottom left, Ron in front of Madison Elementary School which he attended from 1950 to 1956; bottom right, Ron and retired U.S. Air Force nurse Elaine Carlson, who cared for the injured airman in 1967 at Wilford Hall in Texas.

Above, Ron and Eydie Schwerman on a recent trip to Costa Rica; *below,* U.S. Senator Amy Klobuchar visits with Ron during a 2012 Memorial Day Ceremony in Eden Prairie, Minnesota.

CHAPTER 10

Demons Within

Veterans Administration Hospital
Minneapolis, Minnesota

24 October 1967

"We're twenty-five miles out from Minneapolis," reported the pilot of our four-engine Medevac flight. "Nurses, prepare our patients for landing."

"*Almost home*," I thought. My emotions and my stomach flip-flopped between excitement and anxiety. I felt glad to be back in my hometown but anxious about how people I hadn't seen since Vietnam would respond to me. Oh, yeah. One more thing made me VERY anxious. I had to go to the bathroom BAD.

My journey had begun the day before at Wilford Hall Medical Center in Texas. As corpsmen prepared me for transport, a nice but very strict civilian nurse stopped by my hospital room to say goodbye. "Now, you make sure they take care of you up there in Minnesota," she ordered. "If they don't, you have them call me." She said that with a voice of authority, and I could almost imagine her making a very emphatic phone call to a medical colleague a thousand miles north.

Without arms, I'd learned that my comfort, my health, and in some ways my very life, depended on people like this African-American nurse who took it upon herself to see that others did things right. She would even come by my room after I had used the bed pan to make sure the corpsmen had done their jobs. Because I had bed sores, she wanted to make sure they got me clean. Her parting comments reminded me that I was leaving the relative security I had known for the past seven months to face an uncertain world.

Randolph Air Force Base was the first stop along this homeward journey. They loaded me and other patients onto a C-118B Liftmaster, an older, propeller-driven plane. During the flight, a nurse came over to my gurney. I was looking out the window, lost in thought. Perhaps I was trying to anticipate the future. After making small talk, this kind nurse said, "You know, Ron, I've just got the feeling you're going to make it." I took some small comfort in her words, and thanked her.

Leaving Texas, we flew to Scott Air Force Base in St. Louis, where I spent the night in a wing of the base hospital designed for transition patients. I remember feeling like I had to go to the bathroom there, but the trip was so exciting and unnerving that I didn't say anything. I just held it.

Next morning, we took off again and landed at a naval air base in Wisconsin where we exchanged passengers. From there we flew to Duluth Air Base, which I had left in February of 1966 when ordered to Vietnam. As we taxied down the runway, we passed right by the shop where I had worked. I wanted to tell the pilot to stop so I could get out of the plane and run into the shop, shouting, "Hey guys! I'm back!" I wanted to see if Sergeant Wert or any of the other airmen I knew were still there. Then I remembered—I couldn't walk or run. I could have asked the kind nurse to run in and check for me, but I didn't.

We took off again and finally landed at the Minneapolis Naval Air Station[1] near the municipal airport. The air was cool and the sky was cloudy when we landed—a typical late fall day.

An ambulance took me from the plane to the Veterans Administration (VA) Hospital, just five minutes away. Once inside, a lot of people asked me questions and checked me in. Finally, they took me upstairs to the orthopedics ward, but they didn't have my room quite ready, so they parked me on a gurney in the hall. That's where Judie and my friend Neil found me when they came to visit.

I could tell Neil was nervous. We'd been friends since first grade, but he hadn't seen me without my limbs and was trying his best not to say the wrong things. So I decided to enjoy a little humor at his expense. "You've lost a little weight," he blurted out, referring to my thin and emaciated body. I'd also lost some weight by virtue

---

1   Today, this base is operated by the U.S. Air Force Reserve.

of losing my arms and a leg. When I had arrived in Texas, I tipped the scale at around sixty-five pounds. So I decided to pretend that Neil offended me by making a flippant remark about my missing limbs. I gave him a really nasty look for two to three seconds. That caused my friend to backpedal in panic, "Oh, I didn't mean...." Then I started laughing. "It's okay," I told him, "I was just kidding." I am sure that my reaction, coupled with the sight of my missing arms and right leg, affected Neil so profoundly that he shook and completely lost control of his tongue. It took him several minutes to recover.

As for Judie, the reunion went okay despite the grudge I held against her for not coming back to Texas—even though I had told her to stay in Minneapolis. I felt she had left me, but I didn't let it show. Instead, I did a pretty good job of handling my feelings the way I always did, unless I was drunk, by suppressing them. So I said nothing in that hospital hall or during the weeks and months to come about her apparent desertion, because I needed her so badly.

Finally my room was ready. I don't remember meeting any of my doctors or anyone else that late fall day. But one thing I DO remember: I hadn't gone to the bathroom in St. Louis when I needed to. Now cramps gripped my intestines, and I had to go VERY BADLY. When Judie and Neil left, I overcame my shyness and told my nurse Janelle that I had to use the bed pan.

It was no big thing to her. She got me set up, and I finally got relief. I rang the buzzer they'd conveniently located near my right arm stump and Janelle came in to clean me up. Looking at the bed pan she said, "Oh, I see that you've been taking iron down in Texas." She referred to the black color of my stool. I'd been taking supplements because part of my spleen had been removed after the explosion.

That casual observation embarrassed me, but it shouldn't have. She handled my personal hygiene so graciously, as would all of the people at the VA while I was there—whether it was wiping me, holding a urinal, or holding a tissue up to my face so I could blow my nose. They were professional caregivers.

When I left the hospital nine months later, Judie had to do everything for me—including many things I could have done for myself with a little training and effort. But I resisted. As I later learned, doing EVERYTHING for the triple amputee doesn't do anybody's self esteem any good.

Getting better and getting worse

My arrival at the VA Hospital that day in late October began several months of medical procedures aimed at improving my physical condition and allowing me to return home to live with my family. At the same time, my general outlook on life and on the future grew dark, and some internal demons emerged that had haunted me in the years before Vietnam.

The surgeons at the VA did beautiful finish work on the dental reconstruction begun by the surgeons at Wilford Hall. My jaw mandible had healed well, so they built bridges for the bottom and added teeth where I needed them.

At Minneapolis, I continued to battle infection in the bone marrow of my left leg. At one point, someone suggested taking the leg off, and I said, "No, you take that leg off and I'm going with it." It drained for a long time, but they finally got the infection under control. They put a brace on my left leg so that hospital staff—and later my family, friends and aides—could lift me out of my wheelchair, and I could stand. Standing would be good for my whole body. They even fitted the stump of my right leg with a peg like they did in Texas to help me walk. Unfortunately, the inability to adequately address pain in my right leg stump, the shrapnel injury to my left knee, and ongoing sensitivity in my left foot would leave me wheelchair bound.

I had even more surgeries at the VA to revise the stumps of my arms, and they eventually fit me with a set of prosthetic arms. One of the best in the business, Chet Nelson of the Trautman Limb Company, created my artificial arms.[2] But I wore them only occasionally. Most of the time, my new arms hung in the closet of my room at the VA and later in a closet at home. I had heard it was nearly impossible to use prosthetic arms in a wheelchair (which I now know is not true), and I concluded that learning to use them was just too hard.

Tragically, I adopted the same viewpoint about bathroom assists. The VA wanted me to begin using the urinal myself, so occupational therapy fashioned two long plastic pieces, each two inches

---

2   Trautman Limb Company was located downtown Minneapolis.

wide and eighteen inches long. The ends of those pieces fit into bands around the stumps of my arms. The other ends were curled a bit. In theory, I could use these plastic extensions to open my pants, grab the urinal and pee into it. It didn't work very well, but they wanted me to try, and I should have—but I gave up too easily. Judie seemed perfectly happy and willing to take care of me in any way I needed.

The VA did help me do a few things which I might be required to do for myself when my wife was out running errands. Occupational therapy taught me to feed myself with a spork[3] held by a band around the stump of my right arm. They also supplied me with a band and wire I could use to hold and smoke a cigarette. Later, I fashioned a rather elaborate system for loading and lighting a cigarette using my stumps.

Unfortunately, in spite of my earlier embarrassment at others attending to my personal hygiene, I passed on many other opportunities to become more independent.

Meanwhile, I resumed what was my favorite pastime before my injury—drinking. Beer, which had nauseated me when offered in Guam, again became my constant companion, even in the hospital. Neil would bring a six-pack up to my room, and we'd wipe it out. Later, when the VA allowed me to go home on weekends, everything revolved around drinking.

---

3 **Spork** – combination spoon and fork.

In the days and weeks after my return to Minneapolis, I began to experience increased depression and anger. I raged at the protesters filling the streets. I hated the Viet Cong and the way the politicians had conducted this war to which I had contributed body parts. As for the depression, I gradually began to view my situation as hopeless. Despite the VA's progress at fixing me up physically, I saw little prospect for the future and felt the world was passing me by. When depression gripped me, nothing mattered, and when anger consumed me, everything mattered. I could not handle those extreme emotions, so I drank.

Even when someone did something nice for me, I couldn't handle it. I didn't know how. In December 1967, Air Force friends in Texas wanted to fly me and my family down to San Antonio for a Christmas party. We could not leave Minneapolis because the VA had me scheduled for several surgeries. But the mere offer to fly us to Texas floored me. I couldn't imagine the kind of love I was being shown by that invitation, and I simply could not express my love and caring for others in an appropriate manner. I broke down and cried like a baby.[4] My emotions just boiled inside of me, causing all kinds of problems. I drank to calm them.

Occasionally, darker thoughts crossed my mind. No wonder the VA Hospital placed barriers right before the stairs descending from one floor to the next. I asked about those barriers and was told they had been strategically placed to prevent guys in wheelchairs from

---

4   In a similar manner, I broke down and cried upon learning my fellow airman had given Judie and me a gift of $4,000.

trying to kill themselves by rolling down the stairs. It does happen. So, I drank to survive.

Technically, I was discharged from the U.S. Air Force on the day I returned to Minneapolis. Perhaps I should have stayed in the service, moved my family down to Texas, and finished my recuperation at Wilford Hall. The Air Force personnel in Texas were stricter than the civilians at the VA Hospital. I do not blame the VA, but in the Air Force I had to take orders. They gave me wine and beer in Texas to try to put weight on me, but I wasn't drinking regularly. If I had started drinking, they might have caught my addiction earlier and gotten me into treatment. They may also have put artificial arms on me and ordered me to wear them two to three hours a day. If I experienced pain in my stumps, they may have dealt with it. But all this is conjecture.

Now in Minneapolis and more or less on my own, I had pain in my stumps when I tried to wear my artificial arms, but I did not say anything to the VA staff. I just got angry and refused to wear them.

The VA did outfit me with an electric wheelchair before I left the hospital and taught me how to use it. I recall having a hard time learning to drive the wheelchair and was constantly running into the walls, but eventually I got the hang of it. The controls had been positioned further back on the arm of this wheelchair so I could operate them with my stump. Judie and I traveled out to Hopkins where we purchased a used Ford Econoline van with a ramp to transport me and my wheelchair.[5] Eventually I got really good at operating my new wheels, which gave me the ability to go anywhere.

It was too bad I chose to dismiss other tools the VA tried to give me to do more for myself, but I was already headed down the road of settling for less than I could really be or have. My family and friends seemed to accept, and even reinforce, the viewpoint that I was crippled and could do very little for myself. With Judie more than willing to handle any little task for me, I could see no reason to make the extra effort.

In July of 1968, after doing all they knew to do for me physically, the VA discharged me, and I went to live full-time with my family at 118 West Twenty-Ninth Street in south Minneapolis. Judie had moved into the first floor of this rented house soon after my return from Texas. Finally, I had come home.

Soon after leaving the VA, I began having trouble sleeping. I'd dream about plane crashes and rocket attacks. In my dreams, I'd lie flat on the tarmac as ordinance fell around me. Eventually, I'd wake trembling and terrified. Judie would get a wash cloth and wipe off my sweat-soaked body. I had many, many dreams like that.

With this mixture of depression, rage, and horrible apparitions seething beneath the surface, all I wanted to do, now that I was home, was self-medicate. I reasoned that I'd paid my dues. I'd been given a free ticket. I had the money to buy all the alcohol I wanted,

---

5   Before buying that van, Judie would have to bring my dad or Neil along to lift me into our 1959 green and white Chevy. I weighed 85-90 pounds.

and I had Judie to take care of me. What else was there to life than getting drunk?

OUR GOAL: A NEW HOUSE

One thing that did motivate me was finding a different place to live. A tough neighborhood surrounded our rented home, located west of Blaisdell Avenue and north of Lake Street. Moreover, the contractor who built this house in the early 1900s had neither young children nor a handicapped resident in mind.

First off, a big gas stove in the living room provided heat for most of the house. In the winter, that central stove with pipes going up through the ceiling became extremely hot. The thought of our two little kids touching that big stove and getting burned made us very nervous. Then there was the small bathroom and outside steps to the first floor which severely limited my mobility.

Home from the VA on weekends, we made due. With a little help from me, Judie could transfer me onto the toilet. But she had to call my friend Neil to come over and help me into the bathtub. As for the steps, my Uncle Ed Simon, my mother's brother-in-law, built a crude wheelchair ramp to our front door. Life in this older home continued to be a trial, and we dreamed of something better.

Soon after my discharge from the VA hospital, Judie and I began planning a new house. We contacted Harry Jensen, a realtor in Bloomington, who showed us an empty lot which we purchased in the fall of 1968. Next, we hired a contractor, Ken Anderson, to help us design the home and supervise the construction. Ken's men began digging the basement in February 1969.

As earlier alluded, I had plenty of money to drink and to build a house. The federal government had addressed my earlier concerns about how I would support my family. My monthly Social Security disability check combined with my Veterans Administration compensation added up to $1,100 a month. "Good news, Ron," said my financial contact man at the VA. "You'll be making as much as a retired general." In addition, we were eligible for a $12,500 grant from the VA to build a house. My squadron in Vietnam had sent me a total of $6,000, and we had already saved up some money. When we moved into the completed house, we had nearly half the $42,123 house already paid for.[6]

Except for our home building project, however, I had no real goals. Even as plans for our new home took shape, my drinking got heavier and heavier. People tended to explain away my constant inebriation with their pity. "Poor guy. Lost his limbs in the war. Just let him drink." But there was more going on than met the eye. In my depression and rage, I had lost my moral compass. Besides drinking, I smoked dope. Neil and some friends I had made at the VA Hospital brought marijuana over to the house. Neil would also bring pornographic movies that he and I would watch.

Though she didn't tell me until years later, Judie wasn't happy with my drinking. But she did let me know that she was extreme-

---

6   Judie and I were heavy savers. We paid off the house in three-and-a-half years and invited family and friends to a mortgage burning celebration.

ly unhappy about the pot and the dirty movies. That didn't stop me from using or watching. I adopted an "anything goes" attitude for myself, while pronouncing all kinds of moral judgments on everyone else. I would scream at hippies protesting the war, or the politicians and their dishonesty, but I did everything wrong in my private life. I was the biggest hypocrite in the world.

My depravity came to a head at 9:00 p.m. one late summer's eve as I wove crazily up and down our neighborhood in my electric wheelchair. I'd gotten drunk on brandy and headed out the front door without assistance—a stunt I wouldn't have pulled if I'd been sober because I was terrified of that rickety ramp.

In the middle of the street, I came face to face with a police squad car. One of the officers rolled down his window and ordered me to the curb so I wouldn't get hit by the next car to swing down this street. I returned his kindness by yelling and swearing at him and his partner. Among the obscenities, I called them "f—-ing pigs."

So I shouldn't have been surprised when the squad car rounded the block, came up on me from behind at a high rate of speed, and stopped abruptly about two feet from my chair. That scared me to death. The officers got out, arrested me, put me in the back of the squad car and called a paddy wagon to pick up my wheel chair. Then they took me to jail.

The officers charged me with public drunkenness and disturbing the peace. They put me in a cell (instead of the drunk tank), brought me a mattress to soften the hard bench, left the door open (I wasn't going anywhere), and gave me water and pop to drink.

When I needed to relieve myself, they came in with a bucket. In other words, they treated me a lot better than I had treated them.

Next morning, an officer wheeled me before a judge who expressed surprise that I had been charged with disturbing the peace. "I don't know how you could," he said, referring to my missing limbs. Truth is, I was perfectly capable of disturbing the peace, but the judge dismissed that charge and gave me a suspended sentence for public drunkenness.

Before I left the courtroom, the judge instructed me to talk with a counselor about my alcoholism. I still did not think I had a problem. When Judie came to pick me up, I dismissed the incident as a fluke and headed home.

Too bad I didn't listen. The hole I was digging by ignoring my addiction would grow much deeper, destroying my marriage and threatening my daughters' lives.

CHAPTER 11

Our Family Falls Apart

BLOOMINGTON, MINNESOTA

AUGUST 1, 1969

Moving into our newly constructed, three-bedroom home that late summer day should have been a happy occasion. A story in the *Bloomington Sun* newspaper certainly described it as happy. The paper lauded our realtor Harry Jensen who found us a choice lot in a rapidly shrinking Bloomington market; our contractor Ken Anderson, who made the house handicap-accessible; our banker Bob Schave who took a risk by loaning us money on a specially equipped home after other banks had turned us down; and blacksmith-welder George Sunde who fashioned a supporting structure for the hydraulic lift that would lower me into the bathtub.

Because these local men went out of their way to make a livable environment for "a courageous, cheerful young Air Force veteran," reported the newspaper, "Ron, Judie, Pamela, and Rhonda . . . are happily settled in their new home."[1] Sounds like the perfect ending to a perfect day.

In fact, I was crumbling inside. As we began to bring some things into our new house, I remember saying to my wife, "Judie, I'm a sick man." I realized even at that point, before moving in, that the way I was acting was not consistent with how I had been brought up. I didn't feel mentally or emotionally healthy. The anger, the drunkenness, and the language—it wasn't right, and it wasn't normal.

Like I said, I was a sick man, but I couldn't put a name on my illness. I still didn't think I was an alcoholic, despite nights when I would drink three-quarters of a case of beer and half a bottle of vodka—mostly alone. That was another thing out of character for me. I'm actually a very social guy. It's normal for me to be out and involved with people. But here I was, spending more and more time drinking alone in my new house.

Then there was the way I vented on my daughters, who were five and four years old when we moved. If Pam and Rhonda didn't eat their supper, I'd scream and swear at them. "Get to your room," I'd shout. "You're grounded for two days!"[2] I'd feel badly about it later and say to Judie, "Tell them they can come out of their room." But I was inconsistent, and full of anger and rage. Our home was totally

1   Logan, Jim. "Special House Built for Handicapped Veteran." *Bloomington Sun – Richfield Sun – Minnesota Valley Sun* 19 March 1970:23.

2   One time when they were eight and nine I told them that they were grounded until they were twenty-five years old.

dysfunctional. There was no real discipline or proper love. Against this undertow of personal and family turmoil, we moved into our new "happy" home on August 1, 1969.

NO PLANS FOR THE FUTURE

Our family displayed a healthy side at first, as evidenced by the newspaper article. We lived in a nice house, ate regular meals, and wore clean clothes. Judie, who was an excellent housewife, made sure of that.

As for our marriage, we got along well unless I was drinking. Whenever we went somewhere in those early days, she would make it clear that my disabilities did not diminish her love for me. She'd lean over the back of my wheelchair and whisper in my ear, "I'm proud to be out with you." She really tried to be a good wife to a husband who came back without arms and one leg. Looking back, Judie and I could have had a very good and healthy marriage and sex life—even after Vietnam. But my illness worsened.

When we first moved to Bloomington, we didn't have a lawn, so we hired people to lay sod and put in a patio. Every year, we had a big garden in the back yard, and Judie did all the planting and weeding. Summer mornings after breakfast, if I hadn't been drinking the night before, we'd wheel out to the garden and look to see how things had grown overnight.

We even got involved with some hobbies, most of which related to my interests—not Judie's. I did a lot of reading about photography and decided to explore it. We bought the enlarger, the chemicals, the paper and everything else we needed to develop film and make prints. We had a Vivitar 35mm SLR, and everywhere we went, we'd take pictures. **Correction:** *Judie would take the pictures, develop the film and make the prints.* Likewise, we bought a telescope and went outside at night to look at the planets or the moon. Later, I got involved in ham radio, and Judie learned how to solder. I honestly don't know if she enjoyed these hobbies. She usually went along with whatever I wanted.

That said, I had no other goal than to build this new house. I wasn't planning ahead. I wasn't thinking about an education or an occupation. I was getting this big check from the VA so I didn't have to go out and find a job or learn a new trade. As a result, I didn't have anybody pushing me to be better. In retrospect, I think I was in shock, angry about what had happened but not having any idea what a cripple was supposed to do.

Now that my only real goal had been achieved, I didn't do much of anything around our new house. Because of my refusal to wear my prosthetic arms and learn skills that would have made me more independent, Judie had to do almost everything for me and for our family.

Our routine went like this: Judie and I would get up in the morning, have coffee, and smoke a few cigarettes at the kitchen table. In my pajamas, I'd watch Jeopardy or Hollywood Squares on a little nine-inch TV while Judie worked around the kitchen. We'd have eggs and bacon for breakfast. The kids would be at school or out playing, so for lunch we'd have soup and toast. In the afternoon, Judie would go shopping for groceries or run to the BX at the Minneapolis Naval Air station for cigarettes. I almost never went with her. If Judie wasn't out shopping, she was cleaning the house or helping with my personal needs. Occasionally, we'd go for a walk around the block, but it wasn't much of a life.

My main contact with other people came when they stopped by our house.

A GLIMMER OF LIGHT

One afternoon, a month after moving in, we heard a knock at the door. The pastor of a nearby church stood on our front step. We invited him in for coffee. As we talked, we heard another knock. Coincidentally, Pastor Schram from the Missouri Synod Lutheran Church in our neighborhood had also stopped by to get acquainted. I identified myself as a Missouri Synod Lutheran, and the first pastor quickly excused himself.

During his visit, I informed Pastor Schram that I wanted Judie and the kids to start going to church. However, I made it clear I would not be attending with them.

Part of my refusal to attend church had to do with fear. I was already beginning to be afraid of going out in public and being around other people. Out drinking at the VFW, I could handle my fear because I was drunk and in company with other Vietnam veterans. But around other people, I was afraid of how I would react. My fears developed to the point where it made me gag to even think of being seen in public—I was that nervous.

Why I insisted on my wife and children attending church is a mystery to me. I suppose I still had a desire to honor my family's religious tradition, despite the fact that I never attended church in Vietnam. In fact, we rarely attended before my deployment. Judie grew up a Methodist and had committed her life to Christ at a Billy Graham rally before I met her. While dating me, she talked about wanting us to make a Christian home. But I wasn't much interested, and that's where it died.

Nor did I allow her to have any interests outside of my own narrow spiritual experience. While I was in Vietnam, Judie met a Japanese woman married to an Army captain. The woman invited her to attend a Buddhist meeting. I got angry at Judie for going and informed her, "The Bible says you worship God only." But there was nothing in the way I lived my life that supported that viewpoint. My denunciation of Judie's spiritual interests rang hollow with hypocrisy.

So Judie and the kids started going to church. She enrolled Pam and Rhonda in Sunday school, and all three attended Sunday morning worship, while I stayed home. Judie came home from church one day and asked me, "Did you know Jesus was a carpenter?" I didn't say it, but I remember thinking, *"You don't know much about this do you?"* Actually, Judie didn't have much knowledge of the Bible, while I had a basic knowledge from my early years. I could have gotten out the theology books my brother LeRoy had given me and studied so I could answer her questions. I should have become the spiritual leader of our home, but I didn't. I failed miserably.

Funny thing was, shortly after we moved to Bloomington I began reading the Bible from beginning to end. Over the next ten years I would read both the Old and the New Testaments. I was searching for something. What it was, I did not know.

DARKNESS FALLS AGAIN

As time went on, I became more depressed and angry. Reports of the war and how it was being conducted fueled my anger. I became increasingly distrustful of the politicians who led us to believe Vietnam had fewer Communists than it actually did, and who withheld the resources and policies necessary to win the war. Let me be clear—I was not mad at the U.S. Air Force. They just did their job. I directed my anger at politicians—like General Westmoreland, Secretary of Defense McNamara, and President Johnson—for the way they deceived the public. Those on the left who had opposed the war, like Senators McGovern and McCarthy, also angered me.

Every day I'd read the newspaper from front to back, and every night I'd watch the television newscasts. At times the news elated me, like when President Nixon sent troops into Cambodia in May 1970 to rout out the Communists hiding there. But positive reports from the battlefront dwindled. It hit me particularly hard in April of 1975 when the North Vietnamese captured Saigon.

When I went to Vietnam in 1966, I was just doing my time; but now I had to justify my missing limbs. The uselessness of losing over 58,000 American lives in that war and then letting the enemy just walk into South Vietnam—it tore me up.

But it wasn't just the war. Everything seemed unreal to me. The world had changed so much since I left for Vietnam, and I no longer felt a part of it. January 22, 1973 epitomized my struggle. On that day, the U.S. Supreme Court ruled in favor of legalized abortion. I had this creeping feeling that America was losing everything I was brought up to believe in. For the first time I could remember, we were losing wars and now, all of a sudden, it was legal to kill babies. That sentiment may seem ludicrous, considering my own personal depravity, but in both our surrender to the Communists and in the legalization of abortion, I saw America moving toward evil and away from God, in whom I still believed.

It was a dark time for me and for America. I had lost my arms and my leg and was confined to a wheelchair. We'd moved into this beautiful new home, and it hadn't resolved my personal pain and anger. The nation was split over war and civil rights, leaders like Bobby Kennedy and Martin Luther King had been assassinated, and people feared nuclear holocaust. There was a sense of dreariness to life.

I became so anxious and distraught at events in my own life and in the world that one day I asked Judie to shave my head. I had just finished reading the Old Testament book of Job, and that's what the people of the Middle East did when they were distressed—shaved their heads, ripped their clothes and threw dirt in the air.

My anxieties increased markedly in the early 1970s. Afraid to leave the house, I eventually developed a fear of people coming to visit. The very thought would make me physically ill. To deal with the fear, I drank more and more.

Besides alcohol and occasional use of marijuana, I experimented with a variety of prescription and over-the-counter drugs—anything to get high. For instance, I remember trying to get a good buzz off of antihistamines. I was always searching for the best high—like the first time you get drunk. Related to that, I grew increasingly obese. I'd drink heavily one night and the next day I'd eat like a pig, trying to heal or recover from my drinking bout. As a result, I gained a lot of weight.

As destructive as my behavior was to my own health and well-being, its effect on my family proved even more disastrous.

RAISED IN INSANITY

Soon after I arrived back in Minneapolis from Texas, in the fall of 1967, Judie brought our daughters Pam and Rhonda up to the hospital. Pam had seen me in Texas at Wilford Hall, but Rhonda had not seen me and would not have remembered me. She was just four months old when I left for Vietnam. Actually Pam would have been just fifteen months old when I shipped out, so in a sense we were all starting out new in our relationship as father and daughters.

In those early years, we made some good memories—like the time I sat in my wheelchair at the kitchen table with a very hot cup of coffee. I asked Judie for an ice cube and told the girls I was going to make it disappear. "Abracadabra!" I said the magic words and dropped the ice cube in the coffee. To the girls' amazement, it disappeared. "Bring it back again," said Rhonda, and I had to tell her I didn't know the words for that magic trick. As time went on, however, our relationship grew darker and more distant.

Disclaimer: *Much of what I am about to tell you about what my daughters endured over the next ten years comes from Pam and Rhonda themselves. I remember some of this, but not all—either because I was too inebriated or because I've chosen not to remember as a defense mechanism. In any case, I do not doubt these things happened.*

My oldest daughter Pam's earliest memories of me originated on the weekends I came home from the VA Hospital to our rented house at 118 West Twenty-Ninth Street in south Minneapolis. "I remember helping you take off your leg brace in the pantry area, between the living room and the kitchen," states Pam. Three years old at the time, she also remembers how I reacted when our German shepherd puppy "Rex" got hit by a car. "You went out on the ramp and started yelling and swearing," she recalled. That would have been typical of me. Whenever I was extremely sad, it came out in anger.

Pam remembers me sitting at a table by the phone, drinking coffee through a straw. She also recalls me drinking beer with my friend Neil and others who came to visit. My drinking and my volatile temper figures large in her memories of me in those early years. I'll let Pam tell the story in her own words.

Pam: *"We all learned to walk on egg shells and not to say anything until we knew what kind of mood you were* *in. If you were in a good mood, then we'd talk or play around the house. If you were in a bad mood, we'd get out of there for fear we'd say the wrong thing and you'd yell or explode.*

"I knew my life wasn't normal. My best friend Marsha told me that when she looked over at our house she saw a black cloud over it. I think her parents had been talking to her because they were in Alcoholics Anonymous (and knew what was going on). That's why she never wanted to come over and play with me. She always wanted me to come over to her house. At the time, it didn't bother me, but as I got older I knew that wasn't good."

Pam says her best friend's parents sat down with her one day and showed her where they kept their house key, in case she ever needed to come over—even in the middle of the night. "Throughout my elementary years, I don't think you and I ever had a relationship—not a good one anyway," she told me later.

Pam remembers waking up in the middle of the night to the stereo in our living room blasting out Beatles tunes loud enough for our neighbors to sing along. "To this day I know every word of every Beetles song because it happened so often," she states. Pam says I'd be yelling and fighting with Judie over the top of the deafening music. The noise would keep her up all night. Besides being too tired to focus in class the next morning, Pam was often late for school. "I was too scared to come out of the bedroom knowing you were drunk and might still be awake," she explains. When she finally emerged, she'd find a mess of overflowing ashtrays and empty beer bottles.

In junior high, a truancy officer pulled Pam aside and asked her what her home life was like. "I didn't want to reveal everything," she recalls. "He asked me if you drank and I said 'yes,' but I did not tell him about the abuse."

The abuse Pam speaks of included both emotional and threatened physical abuse. "You'd come into our rooms in the middle of the night to wake us up and let us know you were going to kill us," she states. "You'd say to Mom, 'You better get a couple of body bags 'cause you're going to have a couple of dead kids to put in 'em.'" Pam says I threatened to kill her and her sister at least three times over the years.

More often my abuse was emotional but just as damaging to my daughters' future. Pam says I often told her and Rhonda, "You're worthless, and you'll never amount to anything." Judie would try to undo the damage by telling the girls, "Don't listen to him—he's drunk."

My youngest daughter Rhonda was two years old when I came home from Vietnam. Not until she began attending elementary school did she realize other children's dads had arms and legs.

Like her sister, Rhonda retains some very troubling memories of my instability. I'll let her tell this part of the story.

Rhonda: *"My earliest recollection is when we lived in the house in Minneapolis. You saw me sucking my thumb and told me to put it on the table. Then you told Mom to* *cut off my thumb with a kitchen knife. After that I would go hide to suck my thumb.*

"When we moved to Bloomington, I remember counting the nights that I would cry myself to sleep. It got to be such a high number that I couldn't count them anymore. One night I didn't cry, and that was uncomfortable for me. I went into the bathroom, put some water in a Dixie cup, and poured it on my pillow so I could feel the cold water on my face. That helped me go to sleep.

"When you just started drinking, you were fun. We'd come in the front door and through the house with the neighbor kids. You'd 'roar,' and we would laugh and giggle and run out the back door. When you had one or two beers, Pam and I would ask for money to go to the store for candy, and you would usually give it to us. But later, after you had been drinking for a while, you would ask for the money back and get mad that we had spent it. Once, you told us to put our pants down and ordered Mom to take the fly swatter to our butts. You yelled, 'Harder! Harder!' and Mom whispered behind us 'Cry, cry, cry!' so it looked like it hurt, and she wouldn't have to hit us any harder."

Rhonda and Pam looked forward to Christmas and Easter because I didn't drink on those holidays. "When you didn't drink, you didn't yell at us, so we could relax, be happy, and have a good time, explains Rhonda, who recalls the Fourth of July as another happy day. "We'd go into the back yard and watch the fireworks coming from the old Metropolitan Stadium, and you'd pass out sparklers to all the little kids on the block," she said.

As the girls grew older, the good times dwindled. Rhonda tells how I repeatedly interrupted their sleep with macabre games that threatened their lives.

> **Rhonda:** *"When we had to go to bed and you had been drinking, I would always want to sleep with Pam in her big bed, because I knew something would happen. One night, we woke up to the sound of Mom pleading, 'No, Ron. Please, Ron, don't.' We heard you screaming, 'Open the door!' Mom opened our bedroom door, and we were sitting up in bed. Dad, you ordered Pam four or five times to 'Come here!' and when she finally came out you said, 'Put your head on my lap.' Then you yelled to Mom, 'Go buy a couple of little caskets 'cuz we're going to need them tonight.' You made like you were going to cut Pam's head off with your stump. You put your arm up and whacked down really hard and stopped just before you hit Pam—then you rubbed her head.*
>
> *"Other times, you'd call us out of bed into the dining room, and we'd have to stand there stiff like little soldiers for what seemed like hours—not moving.*
>
> *"I remember telling my friends about these nights, and they'd ask me, 'Why don't you just hit him and run*

away? Why don't you push him over?' and I'd tell them,
'No! He's my Dad, and I've got to do what he says.'"

SOMETHING'S GOT TO CHANGE

My fear of leaving the house and of people coming to visit, which actually made me vomit, went on for years. So did my heavy drinking and abuse of my family. Finally, I had had enough. After another night of drinking, at 3:00 a.m. one Sunday in early 1978, I asked Judie to wake the kids—this time for a better reason. "We're going to the VA," I said, blurting it out before I could change my mind. "I want to talk to a psychologist."

Deep down, I wanted help. At that point, I didn't necessarily want to quit drinking, but I definitely wanted to stop acting like an ass and treating people badly. Not long before, I had kicked my own dad out of our house in a drunken rage, and I felt terrible about that.

My family got up and took me to the VA Hospital, where I talked to a psychologist. He asked if I felt depressed. I asked him how he defined depression, and he rephrased his question. "Do you feel like you have the blues?" he asked. "I guess so," I said, but that wasn't necessarily what I was feeling at that moment. I was still drunk. I just wanted the doc to find a way to fix me right then and there.

To my dismay, he told me to come back sober the following Monday, and he arranged for me to see a psychiatric social worker named Joanna Brown. Well, that wasn't the quick fix I expected, but I complied and began meeting weekly with Mrs. Brown. At the same time, the VA doctors put me on an anti-depressant and an anti-nausea drug. As a result, my anxiety and vomiting decreased, and my confidence in going out increased.

We began taking trips. On one occasion, we drove to northern Minnesota to visit Judie's brother Lee. On another trip, we visited Judie's sister Irene and her husband at Park Rapids. We also visited Judie's mother and dad in Milaca and stayed with them a day or two. Since most bathrooms could not accommodate my wheelchair, we purchased a porta-potty to use on overnight trips. I didn't stop drinking, but for the first time in years I was getting out and about.

I also began to socialize with more people. Through the Handi Hams, a club for disabled ham radio operators, I even attended a camp at Maple Lake, Minnesota.

During one of my weekly sessions, Mrs. Brown asked, "What would make you happy?" I replied, "Well, I've always wanted to own a cabin on a lake—but that's something that just wouldn't work." I was thinking of my physical limitations. But Mrs. Brown persisted. "Why don't you and Judie check the paper for cabins for sale, get in your van and drive around looking at them," she said, adding, "You don't have to buy."

Over the course of two or three weeks we looked at several cabins including one on Crow Wing Lake, about twelve miles south of Brainerd. It was located on a wooded lot level enough for me to get down to the lake with my wheelchair and onto a dock. The cabin had electric heat to take the chill out of the air in the spring and fall, and a nice fireplace. The owners wanted $30,000 for the cabin and eighty feet of shoreline. I talked with Judie about it, and she said yes; so in the fall of 1978, we bought our cabin.

Next, we purchased a pontoon and a T-shaped dock so we could easily load my wheelchair onto the pontoon, using a ramp. We also bought a whole lot of fishing equipment that we began to use in earnest the following summer. With the kids out of school, we'd leave Bloomington on Thursday and come back Monday or Tuesday. Virtually every day during these long summer weekends, we'd ride around the lake on our pontoon boat and do some fishing. **Correction:** *Judie would do the fishing. I still wasn't wearing my prosthetic arms.* She caught beautiful sunfish and large mouth bass, and a lot of bullheads which we'd trade to the neighbors for pickled northern pike.

All I wanted to do was spend my weekends at the lake.

TOO LITTLE, TOO LATE

I don't think Judie enjoyed our new pastime. I think she was already gearing up for a split. She had grown increasingly more assertive at times and distant at others. I don't know exactly what was going through her head, but I took a lot for granted at that point in my life. It never occurred to me that she would call it quits.

Even though, when I was raging drunk, I'd say things like, "Why don't you just get out and leave me?" I didn't really have that possibility in my head. Toward the middle of 1979, however, I started picking up signals that something was wrong.

One of these signals came when we were up at the cabin and Judie's sister Connie came for a visit. Connie and Judie took the pontoon out on the lake and talked for hours. I needed help with something and others on shore tried to signal her, but she just ignored them.

A few days later, we sat at our kitchen table in Bloomington drinking coffee and talking about something trivial, when out of the blue I asked her, "You're going to divorce me, aren't you?" I don't even know how I came up with that question. Surprised, Judie looked up and uttered one word, "Yes."

Now it was my turn to be surprised, but not really. When she said yes, it hit me like a ton of bricks. But I must have also sensed this was coming because, as Judie acknowledged her intentions to leave, I felt a weird sense of relief.

We talked for a little while more, and at one point she indicated she might reconsider. "Maybe we could work it out," she ventured, adding, "Do you still love me?" My response to her dashed that small window of hope. "It's just too little, too late," I said, loading all the guilt for this failed marriage on me. I saw clearly that it was my fault, and given my inability to control my drinking, anger, and abuse, I could not imagine making the changes necessary to keep her as my wife. Since that summer afternoon in 1979, I've often wondered whether we might have been able to work it out if I had said "Yes, I still love you." But I didn't.

CHAPTER 12

Independence Breeds Hope

BLOOMINGTON, MINNESOTA

NOVEMBER 1979

When my family moved out, I threw a big party, not to celebrate their leaving but to snub my soon-to-be ex-wife. Judie had just purchased a mobile home in Chaska. On the day she and the girls left our Bloomington house for good, I hosted an early birthday celebration for my daughters. I told Pam and Rhonda they could invite whoever they wanted, and Grandpa Schwerman had promised a birthday cake.

The day of the party, my dad stopped over with the cake. He visited with me upstairs, unaware that his fifteen-and-fourteen-year-old granddaughters and their friends had already launched the real party downstairs by tapping a sixteen-gallon keg supplied by me. Later in the day, I descended to find a basement awash not only in beer but in cocaine. I dutifully voiced my displeasure to Pam and Rhonda about the use of this "hard" drug in our home, but that complaint carried little credence considering my voluminous consumption of alcohol and marijuana upstairs.

*   *   *

Truth was I had given approval to my daughters' substance abuse shortly after Judie announced she intended to divorce me. I hadn't been disciplining them properly before, and with the split looming I gave up all pretense. At our cabin the next weekend, I asked the girls if they had any dope. They eyed me suspiciously, thinking this might be a trap. "No," they said. "Really," I persisted, "I want to smoke some."

"Are you serious?" asked Pam, still distrustful. "Yes," I said. With that, my oldest produced a pipe and filled the bowl with marijuana. "Light it for me and give me a hit," I said. She did, and the three of us smoked it together. Delighted to find I not only approved but would smoke with them, the girls considered it a bonus to get high with their dad without having to dodge the rage that eventually erupted when I drank. Marijuana affected me differently than booze.

On our return trip to Bloomington, with Judie driving and Grandma Duncan in the passenger seat, Rhonda, Pam, and I smoked weed in the back of the van, giggling all the way. Judie knew what was going on but had no power to stop it.

A few weeks later, Pam gave me a new pipe and a bag of weed for my birthday, and the three of us partied often under the slogan, "The family that gets high together flies together." I used my new-found but warped friendship with my daughters as yet another way to lash out at my soon-to-be ex-wife.

After her startling mid-summer announcement, Judie and I had met twice with a marriage counselor at the urging of our pastor. Apparently she still held out hope we could reconcile. It was me who threw in the towel. At our second appointment, I broke down sobbing.[1] While the counselor got a tissue and wiped my eyes, I blubbered, "This isn't going to work. It's over."

* * *

On the day of my daughters' birthday party, it was Judie's turn to cry as she walked through the door of our "happy home" for the last time. By the end of that day, all three of the women in my life had moved out, leaving me utterly desolate.

WHY AM I STILL ALIVE?

I now view my life after my family left as both absolutely misera-ble and the best thing that could have happened to me. That latter viewpoint would take some time to emerge.

---

1 I had also been seeing a counselor at the VA for depression, but the medications prescribed didn't work because I continued to drink.

Despondent, I lay in bed one night and prayed that God would restore my arms. I remember two emotions as I fell asleep that night: hope that the all powerful-God I had believed in since childhood would grant my request, and fear of what I would do if he did. When I woke the next morning still missing my arms, I felt neither sorrow nor relief. Little did I know that God would answer my prayer, in the coming months, in a way I could not imagine.

Despite my desolation, I was not alone—I could not be alone. Judie had done everything for me. Now I found it necessary to employ an aide who agreed to do everything from cooking my meals and driving me to doctor appointments to bathing me, holding my urinal while I peed, and cleaning me after each bowel movement. I knew nothing about hiring aides or having them sign contracts, so my early attempts ended in disaster.

My first aide arrived before Judie left, and Judie trained her. This woman, Nancy, moved in with her two teenage daughters and slowly took over the house. Like Judie, she did everything including feeding me, even though I could feed myself. But I was so dependent and fearful that I didn't know how to object.

To make matters worse, Nancy was a drunk. For a while, it didn't seem all that bad because we just sat and drank together. Then came the manipulation and the theft.

My aide's control and manipulation of me grew worse and worse. At one point, when I had to be hospitalized for a few weeks following a surgery, Mother and Dad came to my house to pick up my mail, and Nancy kicked them out. "You aren't welcome anymore," she told my parents. "Ron and I are getting married, and I'm taking over."

Regardless of my dependence on her, I managed to summon the will to fire Nancy. Mother ran an ad and stayed with me until I could hire two more aides, Frank and Marion. They turned out to be better than Nancy, but not by much. Marian fed a drug habit, and Frank turned out to be a high-functioning imbecile.

While this husband and wife team cared for me, I learned something that shook me to the core and eventually changed my perspective of what had happened to me in Vietnam. One morning early in 1980, Frank drove me to the BX, where I could buy cigarettes and other merchandise at a discount. It was an errand Judie used to run. I had hardly ever accompanied her to the BX.

I rolled inside and was looking at the merchandise when a man walked up to my wheelchair. "I know you!" he exclaimed. The guy did look familiar, but I couldn't place him. He introduced himself as Bob Tillack and proceeded to refresh my memory.

"I stopped to help your wife Judie in 1974 along Cedar Avenue," said Bob. "Her car broke down on the way to the BX." Then I remembered. Judie was headed for the BX when a water hose broke on our 1973 Chrysler Checker Marathon. The engine overheated and steam poured from under the hood. Bob, a retired Navy guy, pulled over to help. He looked at the engine, decided he couldn't fix it, and offered to take Judie to a nearby service station where she could arrange for a tow. Bob then gave Judie a ride to the BX, where he had also been headed, and brought her back to our Bloomington home. "We appreciate your stopping to help," I said when Judie introduced us. "Come in and have a cup of coffee." He accepted my invitation, and we visited briefly before Bob left for his home in Burnsville. I never saw him again until this day, six years later.

"Do you remember me now?" Bob asked. "Yes," I said, thinking his story was over. But it was just beginning.

"That's not the only time we've met," said the big, tall man. He explained how he had served in Vietnam as a Navy corpsman. What he said next took my breath away.

"I picked up your body at Da Nang after a rocket attack," Bob stated. "You were a f—-ing mess and dead as you could be." He described how he found me laying in a pool of my own blood. He said he checked for heartbeat and respiration and found neither.[2] Knowing I was dead, he considered leaving my body at the air base (to be dealt with later) in favor of transporting more wounded. But for some reason, Bob made an illogical decision. "I don't know why; I just threw you into the truck," he recalled.

Bob's story brought back vivid, horrific memories. I began to feel nauseous and sweat poured from my body, but I wanted to hear more.

He told how, when he got to the field hospital a few miles away, he put my body alongside the road and returned to the Da Nang Air Base to pick up more wounded. When he returned to the field hospital, my body had disappeared. He was shocked to find out later that I was alive and in surgery.

---

2   Apparently I had not made a sound, though in my mind I was screaming bloody murder to let the corpsman know I was alive. *See Chapter 1.*

As Bob finished his account, so many thoughts swirled through my mind, and I felt physically ill. All I wanted to do was to get out of the BX. I made some excuse and headed for the door. Before I left, the ex-corpsman gave me his phone number and offered to get together at a later date.

I didn't follow up his invitation until years later. When I finally called, the number had been disconnected. I have so many questions about his incredulous story: What compelled Bob to pick me up that day when he was convinced I was dead? And why didn't he bring up our encounter in Vietnam when he met Judie and me back in 1974? I may never know.

One thing I do know, something or somebody wanted me to live.

"In my distress, I called to the Lord . . . he reached down from on high and took hold of me; he drew me out of deep waters. He rescued me from my powerful enemy, from my foes, who were too strong for me . . . he brought me out into a spacious place; he rescued me because he delighted in me." Psalm 18: 6a, 16-17, 19 (NIV)

My emancipation

As I said, Frank and Marion turned out to be only slightly better than my first aide. So it was good timing when my nephew Jon

Knutson[3] strolled up the walk to my Bloomington house in the spring of 1980. I used to babysit Jon as a kid, and he'd come out to Bloomington for a visit with his favorite uncle. "How are things working out?" he asked. "Not great," I replied. "Marion is passed out half of the time, and Frank is kind of a dork."

"Why don't you fire them?" inquired Jon. Then he dropped a bombshell. "I'll be your aide." Thinking he might be half serious, I asked Jon if he knew this job involved everything from bathing me to wiping my butt. Jon said he did, but I think he was already planning what he would do to fix me. In his mind, I wasn't going to sit on my drunken ass for the rest of my life.

We went inside, and I told my current aides their services were no longer needed. Jon moved in immediately. Frank and Marion stayed for more two weeks while they looked for work.

Jon was a mover and a shaker. He pushed hard for me to be more independent. Sometimes I'd tell him to back off, but secretly I wanted Jon to challenge me to do more.

Jon implemented his emancipation plans immediately. Judie and I had bought a large aquarium, and Jon moved another fish tank into my house. He convinced me to go with him down by the Mississippi River to find big rocks for these aquariums. When we reached to the steep bank, I told Jon, "There's no way I can get down by the river—I'll just wait up here."

---

3   Jon Knutson is the son of LeRoy Knudson, my half brother. He had served in the Marine Corps on a ship off the coast of Vietnam where they brought many of the dead. "They were piled up like logs," he said.

"No, you won't!" exclaimed Jon. "You're going with me." He grabbed the handles of my wheelchair and pushed me down the bank, over hills and through gullies until finally we stopped at the river's edge. It was one of the wildest rides I've ever taken and my first taste of the independence Jon intended for me.

My new aide also insisted we buy season passes to the community swimming pool at Ninetieth Street and Portland Avenue. We spent many warm afternoons there during the summer of 1980. Muscular Jon would take me out of my wheelchair, put me in an inner tube and also have me swim on my back while holding me up.

Insisting I could do more for myself, Jon rigged up my bathroom so I could shave, brush my teeth, and use the toilet all on my own. Remember, this was without arms—I just used my stumps with the help of mechanical devices Jon set up. At bath time, he'd get me in the tub, fill it with water, and give me a wash cloth and soap. "You can wash your face," Jon said. Then he'd get me out of the bath, give me a towel, and tell me to dry myself as much as I could. He'd take care of the rest.

At first, Jon's pushing me to be more independent irritated me a little. After all, for the past thirteen years someone had done absolutely everything for me. But I soon began enjoying the idea of tackling whatever tasks my nephew gave me, and I felt a real sense of accomplishment whenever I mastered something like brushing my teeth, which took a long time to perfect.

Every day involved a lot of work and sweat, but every day I learned something. At the end of each day, I would be so exhausted that I'd fall asleep as soon as my head hit the pillow. Neither Jon nor I would wake until 10:00 a.m. the next morning.

Jon loved my mother—after all, she was his grandmother, but Mother and Jon disagreed vehemently about his pushing me to be more independent. "Ronnie can't take care of himself," she'd say, revealing her over-protective attitude. Jon insisted, "Ron already does many things for himself and can learn more if he's willing." As it turned out, Jon was right.

Whenever Jon challenged me to do more, I'd cooperate. He'd constantly be pushing or pulling me into something new, and for some reason I didn't fight him. It was like being in a canoe in the middle of a stream without a paddle and just riding with the current. Sure, it was a little scary (especially careening down the bank toward the Mississippi River), but somehow I knew I was heading in the right direction.

I did let Jon know there were limits, and he respected me. We often went out to eat at a restaurant or to drink at a bar, and being in a public space, the agoraphobia would occasionally return. "If you ever have a panic attack," Jon told me, "all you have to do is say *crow* (our code word), and I'll get you out of there." And he was true to his word; I think Jon understood me.

Encouraging me to ask the VA for another set of arms was perhaps the biggest thing my nephew did to propel me to greater independence, and it proved to be God's answer to my earlier prayer to restore my upper limbs.

Shortly before Jon arrived on the scene, the staff at the VA Hospital had weighed me for the first time in years. I had tipped the scale at 238 pounds. That probably was comparable to a person with arms and legs who weighed 300 pounds. Shocked, I asked to speak to a dietician. She eventually helped me lose over 100 pounds. I had little problem losing weight for two reasons: I was a heavy smoker, and I cut back quite a bit on my beer intake. (Unfortunately I replaced a lot of my drinking with smoking marijuana.)

When Jon suggested I try artificial arms again, I still weighed over 200 pounds. My first set of arms, made in 1968 and promptly hung in the closet, no longer fit me. At Jon's urging, I went to the VA and asked to be scheduled for an amputee clinic—the gateway to being fitted with new prosthetic limbs.

At the clinic, a doctor questioned my motivation. "Why should we give you arms now?" he asked. "We already gave you a set, and you wouldn't wear them." Emboldened by Jon's encouragement, I stated, "I want to try again, and I think I can do it this time."

The VA finally decided to grant my request for new arms. By late summer of 1980, I wore those prosthetics regularly and experienced a level of independence I had not had since Vietnam. Jon saw to it that I did. He'd even make me go down to the basement where we kept a keg, fill a pitcher with beer, and bring it back upstairs.[4] Before I had this second set of artificial arms, he pushed me

---

4 The contractors who built my house in 1969 installed an elevator so I could access the basement with my wheel chair.

hard to learn how to do what I could on my own. With my new arms, he urged me to do even more.

Wearing and learning to manipulate my artificial limbs did not come easily. Occasionally a cable would break, and I'd have to re-adjust everything. Also, my stumps had worn down with age and wearing my new arms for very long resulted in major pain. The prosthetic limbs created a big red spot on my right stump, and I was afraid it would break through the skin. But with Jon's support and attention to my needs in those early days and weeks, I could bear the break-in period.

I recall one night the two of us went out drinking and flirting with girls at the Vikings Bar in the Seven Corners area when John saw I was struggling. "What's going on?" he asked. "This right arm is killing me," I told him. Jon came over and removed my artificial arms right in the middle of the bar crowd. "Just sit there with them off for a while," he advised, watching me close to see if I would *crow*.

Later that night, when I'd already turned in, Jon rubbed my neck and back to smooth out the muscles I used to wear and oper-ate the arms. Later, I learned some exercises that helped to relieve the muscle strain.

Jon and I parted ways in the fall of 1980; but in only a few months, by pushing me to do more for myself, he had helped me achieve a measure of freedom I had not experienced in years. By encouraging me to get and wear a second pair of artificial arms, he opened the door to new opportunities that would present them-selves in the future—like learning to drive.

Though I could not verbalize it at the time, I gained a sense of hope that life would be better in the future. How that would take place, I did not know. I still drank and smoked dope and there remained many things, like my tendency to explode in anger, which needed work. But at least my life appeared to be moving in a positive direction.

My newfound independence became an important key to my recovery from the deep physical and emotional pit I'd dug in the years following my injury. I wish I could say my recovery followed a straight line up, out of that pit. It did not.

CHAPTER 13

Diagnosis PTSD

BLOOMINGTON, MINNESOTA

JULY 11, 1981

That next summer, I threw a big Independence Day party in my suburban back yard. This patriotic theme seemed appropriate for a party scheduled for a Saturday evening, one week after our national mid-summer holiday. Secretly, I may have wanted to mark my status as a single man—my marriage to Judie had legally dissolved June Fourth of the previous year. Or I may have wanted to trumpet my newfound ability to do more for myself. I could have been celebrating all of the above. In any case, I threw a huge bash that ended in disaster.

My new aide Michael had a talent for cooking. He was also manipulative and spooky. At one point he saw me stuffing checks in envelopes and putting stamps on them. It was a lot of work with my relatively new arms, and I complained about it to Michael. "Why don't you give me power of attorney," he replied. "Then I can do all this for you." A light bulb went on in my head, and I said firmly, "No, I'm not going to do that." I saw Michael's offer as a ploy to gain access to my bank account.

That was typical of my thinking at the time. I was smoking a lot of marijuana and the trauma of my Vietnam service, coupled with the bad experiences I had had with earlier aides, left me extremely paranoid. Michael's bizarre antics pushed me to the brink. He would come up behind my wheelchair and scare the heck out of me, or he'd arrange the food on my plate in a fancy design. When I'd say, "Michael, you don't have to do this...," he'd say. "Oh, really?" Then, he'd pick up the plate and shake it so hard that the food ended up in a jumbled mess. Because of strange behavior like this, I lived in fear of him. But I'll say it again: Michael was a talented cook and good at setting up parties.

So I bought a pig, and Michael roasted it in the back yard. We set up a big party tent and invited around 150 people. My guests included doctors, nurses, social workers and a lot of other staff and veterans I'd met at the VA, as well as family—my parents, my aunt, and my cousins. We hired a band to play on the patio; everyone was dancing and having a good time, despite the hot and humid weather.

Mid-way through the party, the Bloomington police knocked on my front door.

A guest opened the door and came back to find me. "The cops are here," he yelled over the music. "Bring 'em back here," I said. That was my first mistake. Three officers filed through the house and out onto the crowded patio. The lead officer approached me. "Neighbors are complaining that the noise is too loud," he told me. "You're going to have to shut the party down."

"Can't we just stop the music," asked one of my guests. "No, said the officer flatly. "The party is over." As he said this he put his foot on one of my tires. "Hey, get your foot off my wheel chair! I growled, adding, "That's part of my body."

"Oh, tough guy, huh?" said the cop. That was it. The police officer could have handled the situation better, but I alone allowed that last comment to light my fuse. As it burned toward inevitable explosion, I nursed the flame along. "I come back to this country after losing my limbs protecting its freedom and THIS IS HOW I GET TREATED!" I fumed. Then my seething rage burst into a great physical display of rage. I wheeled around, sped up the ramp and into the house. There was a big cake on my dining room table, decorated like an American flag. I got so damn mad that I raised my hook and brought it down into the cake, splattering frosting everywhere.

The police overreacted, too. They had been called many times before to this address to deal with my drunkenness. Maybe they were angry about being called again. In any case, they escalated the confrontation by mistreating my guests as they tried to break up the party. Among other things, they manhandled Dad and pushed him out the front door. Also, a pregnant guest received a blow (accidentally or intentionally) to her stomach, sending her to the hospital with labor pains.

In the middle of all this, I headed down the hall to my bathroom to discharge the liquid remnants of my beer consumption. When I came out, a female cop blocked my way. "I'm not letting you through until you tell me your name," she declared.

"I'm not telling you my name," I retorted and rammed my wheelchair into the officer, pushing her over like a floor lamp. The whole scene descended to chaos.

Eventually all of my guests left, and the police ticketed me for drunkenness along with other violations. Mercifully, they did not charge me with assault on an officer or arrest me. I considered suing the police department and hired a well-known local lawyer to help me sort things out. In the end, he decided there was not enough of a basis for the suit, and I paid a fine. The story of the police raid ended up on WCCO-TV with me accusing the police of "acting like the Gestapo" and the Bloomington police chief having his say as well.

One good thing did come from this Independence Day blow out. To this point, I had not admitted my alcoholism. I'd suspected and toyed with it, reading articles in *Psychology Today* and even defending Judie when my mother bad-mouthed her for divorcing me. "I don't think it's all Judie's fault," I protested. Even then I realized I had done my share to drive her out of the house.

But now I came face-to-face with the thought that this entire mess would not have happened if I had been sober. As time passed and I mulled it over, I concluded that the party would have ended very differently if I hadn't been drunk. I tried to rationalize that it was muggy that day and tempers were short on both sides. But in the end, those excuses didn't work. It had to do with my drinking, and I knew it.

ANOTHER PUZZLE PIECE

About this time I began hearing the term PTSD[1] (post-traumatic stress disorder) used in reference to my uncontrolled anger. One of the guests at my Independence Day party was Clayton Bawden, a counselor at the Vets Center in St. Paul. I'd become acquainted with Clayton when I got my second set of arms. For several months I met with him to address psychological problems related to learning the use of my new prosthetics.[2] Clayton was working on his PhD and the subject of his doctoral thesis was PTSD.

Clayton thought I had PTSD, and at first I didn't believe it. "Clayton," I argued, "I was a mechanic on an Air Force base, not out in the jungle fighting hand-to-hand with the Viet Cong."

"You don't have to be in the jungle to have PTSD," insisted Clayton, noting that I had been in Vietnam for an entire year before my

---

1 See *Appendix 1—Help for PTSD-Afflicted Vets for a brief discussion of the disorder and what families can do to help.*

2 It was Clayton who first caused me to wonder if I might be an alcoholic. "Do you think you would have done the same thing if you were sober?" he asked after my Independence Day party fiasco.

traumatic injury. "You were under constant threat of getting hurt or killed in a mortar attack."

Eventually, Clayton convinced me that the extreme anger and depression I exhibited, together with my continuing nightmares of rocket attacks and planes crashing, pointed to PTSD. According to my counselor, I used alcohol and marijuana to medicate this condition.

Now, I must point out that PTSD didn't cause my drinking. I began drinking long before enlisting in the U.S. Air Force. But it certainly made sense that my drinking would exacerbate the PTSD, numbing my real feelings and uncovering a lot of buried anger and rage that I acted out in some very destructive ways.

According to Clayton, the VA should have given me more help when I got back from Vietnam. "They gave you antidepressants but no counseling," he told me in disgust. He was at least half right. On the one hand, no one asked anything about what was going on inside my head. On the other hand, I hid everything from everybody, so how could they know. If someone asked how much I drank, I'd say, "Oh, a few beers . . ." when in fact I was drinking fifteen to twenty beers a day and a half quart of vodka or bourbon two to three times a week.

At that time, medical personnel had just begun to understand and diagnose PTSD, so Clayton made some enemies at the VA with his different ideas. Some staff liked him, but others viewed him as a trouble maker, especially when he criticized their commonly accepted practices.

Clayton was, in fact, a bit of a manipulator, using our friendship for his own purposes. At one point, after our counseling sessions had ended, he asked me to write letters to various senators, congressmen, governors, and heads of the VA. He'd help me word the letters and tell me, "Now print ten copies, sign them, and mail them to this list of people." He was using me to further his agenda, a fact I didn't totally understand until later. I reasoned, "Whatever he's doing has got to be good." So I agreed to help him.

I suppose I identified with Clayton since we had similar experiences and handicaps. Although he was twenty to thirty years older, Clayton had been a pilot in the U.S. Air Force. After his discharge, Clayton married and fathered two daughters. He worked in a bank until one day he dove into a pool, hit the bottom and broke his neck. The resulting paralysis ended his banking career and eventually his marriage.

Clayton lived with his mother who helped care for him into her 90s, along with a parade of aides he employed over the years. Now you understand my affinity to him.

WHY I BELIEVE WHAT I BELIEVE

After Clayton finished counseling me, we continued as friends and regularly went out to dinner or to have a beer or two. Occasionally, we'd go over to his house and I'd smoke a little marijuana while Clayton had a cocktail. So he probably wasn't the one to address my alcoholism—although he helped me become aware of it.

The other thing Clayton's friendship did for me was to strengthen my faith and spur me to investigate why I believed what I believed. As I've stated, my parents raised me as a conservative Lutheran. As long as I can remember, I had believed in God and the gift of his son, Jesus Christ, on the cross. I even read the Bible from Genesis to Revelation in the 1970s, but I could not articulate my beliefs. Furthermore, the way I lived my life bore little relation to my professed faith.

As I spent time with Clayton, a professed agnostic,[3] he constantly challenged me to defend my beliefs. We both enjoyed talking and debating a variety of topics. When the question of faith came up in our conversations, I told my friend that I believed in God and that I was a Christian. He would reply, "If you'd have been born in India, you'd be a Hindu or if you'd been born in Iran, you'd be a Muslim. You were born in America, so you became a Christian." Truth was I lacked theological knowledge and had no answer for Clayton's claims that my religious beliefs simply identified my heritage. He'd pepper me with one question after another that begged an answer if my faith had any credence. Then he'd look at me with a cocky smile as if to say, "Answer THAT ONE, Ron."

At approximately the same time, I hired a new aide, Anne, who belonged to the Mormon Church.[4] She drove me to dinners with

---

3   **Agnostic** – a skeptic as to the existence of God or man's ability to know him.
4   Known formally as the Church of Jesus Christ of Latter Day Saints, the Mormon Church is considered by many Christians to be a cult.

Clayton. While Clayton and I debated the existence of God, Anne tried to convert me to Mormonism.

Looking back at this important time in my life, I believe God was pushing me to learn more about him. I had a Mormon aide that I couldn't show where she was wrong and an agnostic friend whose questions I could not answer. So I started to dig.

A friend of my brother LeRoy owned a Christian book shop down on Chicago Avenue and Forty-Sixth Street, so I went there to buy some Bible commentaries. My brother brought me some books as well, and eventually I purchased the complete works of Martin Luther, including his interpretation of the Bible from Genesis to Revelation.

Besides wanting answers to the questions of my friends, Anne and Clayton, I found myself starving for a deeper understanding of my faith. As I read, it became more and more real to me. Tears came to my eyes as my heart acknowledged that what I was reading had actually happened. I began to see Christianity in a totally different light.

Before, there was no life in my faith. It was just a story I would probably defend to the death, but I didn't know why I believed it. I didn't comprehend it as something that had, in fact, taken place. Now I knew that Jesus Christ was really God and understood what his hanging on the cross 2000 years ago meant to all mankind.

I began to consider what the Bible said about my personal failures—my getting drunk, raising hell, treating Judie like crap, and psychologically abusing my daughters. I started to understand that

I was indeed a sinner and that the Son of God had come to earth to die on the cross for sinners. He came to die for me.

None of this happened overnight. It took months of reading the Bible, Luther, and other commentaries—anything I could get my hands on—for my faith to come alive. But, over the period of about one year in conversation with Clayton and Anne, I gained a strong belief in the God to whom I had been introduced as a child. In reality, He guided me to Himself through my agnostic and Mormon friends.

"Blessed is he whose transgressions are forgiven, whose sins are covered. Blessed is the man whose sin the Lord does not count against him and in whose spirit is no deceit." Psalm 32:1-2 (NIV)

STILL MAKING POOR CHOICES

Unfortunately God's becoming real to me didn't change my bad behavior overnight. I continued to make wrong choices. Before Anne signed on as my aide we had begun a sexual affair that continued for several years. After hiring her as my aide, she moved into my house with her young children—one of whom was severely disabled. Twice Anne and I got engaged but never married.

Several months into our relationship, Anne decided to convert to Christianity. She had gone over to my church to talk with Pastor Schram about membership, and I was delighted to learn that her children would be baptized. But whenever the pastor came to the house to give me communion, our live-in arrangement raised some questions. We knew it wasn't right, and the pastor wasn't dumb. So simply to assuage our guilt, we got engaged. It was hypocrisy on both our parts, and we soon broke off the engagement. But we continued to live together.

A couple years later, we again became engaged. Feeling pressure from the church, Anne and her children had moved out. However, we still maintained our sexual affair and she continued to be my aide. This time, I had bought Anne a ring. We had set a date and people in the church were calling to congratulate us. Then my attorney issued some sober words of warning.

"Under no circumstances should you marry this woman," he advised. "She has a disabled daughter and a lot of medical bills. If you marry her, her creditors will come after you, and it will wipe you out."

That put me in a bind. I had already proposed to Anne and everyone knew we were engaged, but my lawyer had advised me not to marry her.

It took some time for me to work up the courage to talk with Anne. Meanwhile, her son Shawn let slip a comment his mom had made to him. "As soon as you two get married," said the boy, "she plans to go out and buy a new Subaru." That really bothered me. I didn't appreciate Anne going behind my back, and it lent some credence to what the lawyer had said about my vulnerability.

Finally I told her, "Anne, this isn't going to work." Judging from her reaction, she knew immediately what I meant. Things were never the same after that, and right away we decided I had better get another aide.

Despite my poor choices, my relationship with Anne (and my friendship with Clayton) had helped put in place another puzzle piece to my recovery—the discovery of my faith. But I still needed help putting that faith into action, as evidenced by my behavior with Anne and my continued love affair with alcohol.

Even when Anne and her kids lived with me, I would drink and smoke dope on the sly. With their moderating influence gone, I fell back into a pattern of heavy alcohol and drug abuse. Then I caught a glimpse of myself in a mirror and saw my addiction for what it really was.

CHAPTER 14

Getting Sober

Bloomington, Minnesota

For years I had toyed with the idea that I might be personally responsible for the chaos in my life, and that my habitual intoxication played a big role.

One horrifying experience brought me face-to-face with my culpability, and I saw my alcohol and drug abuse for what it really was—an evil addiction. I acquired a bag of marijuana from a former aide who tried to sell it to me at a low-ball price. When I said no, the dealer got mad and walked out the door. "You keep it," he said over his shoulder. "I don't want it." That should have warned me off. Instead, I smoked some of the dope right then and there. A few hours later, I smoked more.

I remember being in the kitchen and turning my head toward the microwave. What I saw scared me to death. A demonic image stared back at me from the glass door of the appliance. In my mind, I was convinced of two things: that image was the anti-Christ and the anti-Christ was me. *"If I really am the anti-Christ,"* I reasoned, *"then I am doomed to hell forever and nothing can be done about it."*

In a panic, I put down my pipe immediately and swore to God, "If I come out of this alive, I will never smoke marijuana again."

I fell asleep that night but remained high for more than twelve hours. Looking at myself in the bathroom mirror the next morning, it still seemed like I had horns. I didn't say a thing as I rolled into the kitchen where my aide was cooking breakfast. I wanted to see what she said. "Your hair is mussed up," she observed. "It looks like you have angel's wings." My aide's remark helped me to rationalize the apparition in the microwave door, as did a conversation with my counselor/friend Clayton. He theorized the marijuana had been laced with angel dust.[1] It helped to know I may have just been hallucinating, but Clayton's next comment was sobering. "Occasionally we see veterans who get stuff like that and never come out of it," he stated. "They end up in a nursing home for the rest of their lives."

This should have been my turning point, but despite my scare and Clayton's warning, I broke my promise and began smoking dope again.

---

1   **Angel Dust or PCP** (phencyclidine) – a long-lasting recreational drug producing hallucinogenic and other more damaging effects.

Finally, twenty years, nine months, and six days after my injury in the rocket attack at Da Nang Air Base, I hit bottom. Alone at home on Monday evening, November 30, 1987, I took a few hits from a pipe. I may have been drinking, too—I just don't recall. What I do remember is suddenly feeling very, very remorseful for my failed marriage to Judie and my recent break-up with Anne. My daughters had dropped out of high school and were on a fast track to nowhere. Divorced and in the midst of a custody battle for her children, my older daughter Pam had recently checked into a local hospital for treatment of cocaine addiction. My younger, Rhonda, was out in California doing drugs. She'd be higher than a kite when she called to tell me that little worms were coming out of the carpet. My own drinking had landed me in trouble with the police several times. To put it bluntly, I had made a mess of my life and the lives of everyone else I had touched.

I became overwhelmed with guilt and regret. I do not think I cried at first, but that evening my whole sordid past played before me like a movie on the big screen.

Regret quickly turned to anger. I saw very clearly that my use and abuse of alcohol and drugs had accounted for the stench of insanity and destruction emanating from my life. *"I'm drunk or high on drugs, so I don't make good decisions with women, and I do things that hurt others,"* I admitted in disgust.

Then another thought hit me: *"I've had enough of this! I'm fed up with all the pain and suffering I have caused other people and myself."*

What happened next proved to be the real turning point. I went down the hall, opened a safe in my bedroom closet, and pulled out a large bag of marijuana. Unlike my "free" dope, this bag had cost me several hundred dollars. I rolled into my bathroom and began flushing it down the toilet. By now, I was most certainly weeping. I know I felt intense anger, regret, and sorrow—all at the same time.

Then I went to bed.

"The bottom is a wonderful place to be.
That's where the change comes."
–*Mariano Cashlan, a Mayan Indian*

SPILLING MY GUTS

The following morning, I got up and immediately called Pastor Schram. "I need to talk," I told him. He arrived on my doorstep within five minutes. Pastor Schram had been my spiritual leader for over eighteen years, but I had not let him into the secret places of my life. All that changed over the next hour and a few cups of coffee. I told the pastor my whole sordid story and concluded by admitting to him, and to myself, that my drinking and drug abuse had gotten me into fights and in trouble with the police, even before I enlisted in the Air Force. As we visited at my kitchen table, I broke down and cried like a baby. I viewed my whole life as a sewer of problems I'd caused myself and others, and I was beginning to regurgitate all this pain and suffering. Instead of expressing shock, Pastor Schram listened patiently and offered me the true encouragement and the support I needed to continue. At one point during my confession, the doorbell rang. He got up, opened the door, and told my visitor firmly, "Ron is busy right now. You can call him later."

After regaining my composure and with the pastor at my side, I got on the phone and called the Veterans Administration Hospital. I was ready to admit that I needed help with my addiction. The VA put me through to the head of the alcohol and drug treatment program on one of its wards—a man named John. After checking my records, John and I determined it would be too difficult for me, as a triple amputee, to participate in the VA's in-patient program, which began at 6:00 a.m. every day and had no provision for helping me get dressed and start the morning early. At John's urging, I contacted Fairview Southdale Hospital in Edina where my daughter Pam was undergoing inpatient treatment. I made an appointment to be evaluated by a counselor, who eventually enrolled me in an outpatient treatment program with the flexibility to accommodate my disability.

Having admitted my alcoholism to my pastor and to the counselor, I remained sober for the entire month of December and entered treatment on January 4, 1988.

The outpatient treatment program met four nights a week, Monday through Thursday. My aide dropped me off at 6:00 p.m. and picked me up four hours later. The initial treatment lasted six to eight weeks and the aftercare program lasted six to eight months. I met with other alcoholics in groups to hear lectures, watch movies, and talk among ourselves as we learned about our addiction. Occasionally, the counselor would confront us, or we would confront each other if we felt somebody in the group was not being truthful. Sometimes recovering alcoholics would come and talk to us about how they were doing after several years of sobriety.

I also met with my daughter Pam for family therapy. My counselor advised Pam to confront me about my mistreatment of her and Rhonda as they were growing up. "What did your dad do to you?" the counselor asked. Pam told how I had verbally abused them by yelling and swearing in the middle of the night when they were trying to sleep. She said they could understand my anger because of coming back from Vietnam without arms and legs. "Yes," I replied, "but that didn't give me a right to do what I did to you."

Pam did not reveal to the counselor the depth of my mistreatment, but we have talked at length about it since then.

In treatment, I learned how drugs and alcohol affect our bodies and our brains. For instance, I learned that when an addict drinks or gambles it generates chemicals in the brain that produces pleasure; however, maintaining the same pleasure requires drinking more or betting more each time.

I also studied co-dependency. I learned that a husband can be a full-blown alcoholic and his wife a teetotaler, but she can actually enable his drinking. She might help him into bed when he can't walk, clean up his vomit, or call his boss to say he can't come in to work. Despite the physical and emotional abuse, a co-dependent enabler still gets something out of a relationship—familiarity. In Judie's case, she had clothes, food, a house to live in and bills that were paid. To leave (which she finally did) would have been to move from the familiar to the unfamiliar. It's a scary situation, especially when you have two young girls to raise. A lot of co-dependency occurs because the enabler does not know what will happen and what is possible if they leave—so they stay.

Understanding this, I began to see my marriage with Judie, and even my relationship with Anne, in a new light.

New level of independence

During the treatment program, I reached another turning point. In the spring of 1988, I contacted the VA and told them I wanted to learn how to drive. Chicago had the nearest VA program for triple-amputees, and I would have to bring an aide with me to the Windy City for several weeks in order to participate in that program. Instead, I turned to the Courage Center,[2] a non-profit organization based in Golden Valley, Minnesota, which is dedicated to training disabled people to do everyday life. It draws people from all over the United States and other countries who want to learn to live independently.

---

2 The Courage Center ran the Handi-Hams ham radio club I had belonged in the 1970s.

A Courage Center staff member named Steve Quinn evaluated me and concluded, "We can teach you to drive, Ron." But Steve also warned me that he was a mover and a shaker. "I don't play around with my driver's training," he said. "You're going to get into the van the very first day and drive." He was true to his word.

During our first session, he took me down to the Courage Center garage where he kept the van I would drive. The equipment he used to accessorize the van to teach disabled people like me was portable. He could set it up to accommodate whatever disability his students had. My setup was identical to a quadriplegic. He also had a set of brakes on the passenger side, so he could stop us if need be.

When he had adjusted the equipment, Steve started the van. "Okay Ron," he said. "Shift into drive and let's go out of the garage." It had been twenty-one years since I had driven anything, and with my artificial limbs the very prospect of taking control of the vehicle scared and intimidated me. But Steve remained calm. He directed me out onto the street and down the road a bit. Then he instructed me turn left into a church parking lot where we practiced adding gas, hitting the brakes, turning in circles and other basic moves. That was my first driving lesson, and I still can't believe this guy took me out on the road in traffic. He had guts.

I took driving lessons twice a week at the Courage Center, and the VA agreed to pay for them. After sixteen lessons, Steve rode with me to a nearby driver's exam station, and I passed the test with a score of ninety-two. I still keep the examination form to remind me of this milestone in my life.

I was happy. It was good for my independence and for my self esteem to have my license after so many years of depending on others to drive me where I needed to go. But I still didn't have a vehicle equipped so that I could drive it, so my aide drove me to Associated Leasing in Burnsville.[3] I presented them with paperwork from Steve, which detailed the adaptive equipment I needed to drive, such as wide-angle side mirrors, hand controls for brakes and gas, and a steering wheel with features like a steering knob and zero effort steering. From Associated, I ordered a van with a lift and a lowered floor so that I could roll my wheelchair right into the driver's side and lock it in place at the same level as if I were sitting in a standard seat.

It took about two months for the customized van to arrive. A good friend, John Waseleski, drove my old van (which I traded) to Associated and drove my new van home. He put it in the garage and that's where it sat for a couple of days. Truthfully, I feared driving it. Soon, however, a member of my church, who was also a recovering alcoholic, stopped by for coffee. (I think our pastor put him up to it.) After downing a cup, he said, "Let's go for a ride." I had no excuse. We went out to the garage and I drove the van—just around the block, but I did okay. That was twenty-four years ago,

---

3   Associated Leasing is now Rollx Vans of Savage.

and I've been driving ever since on residential streets and on the Interstate. But I needed that "kick in the pants" to get started.

Slowly, slowly I gained self confidence because of this new level of independence and also because of my treatment for alcoholism. I felt less and less shame as I understood more about the disease which had haunted me since youth, and as I took responsibility for my past.

I could not graduate from initial treatment until I had accomplished the first five steps in the twelve-step program of Alcoholics Anonymous (AA). The Fifth-Step required me to go before another person, a friend, a pastor, or a counselor to confess the evil in my life. I'll be honest. This was difficult for me. I've done so many wrong things. Before taking this step, I listed my sins on paper to help me remember all of them when I went before my confessor, an Episcopal priest.

During the hour we spent in his office I confessed some things that would have made the devil blush. My admissions of guilt didn't faze him. He'd probably heard even worse, but these were things that caused me shame. I look back on that event as a way of purging all the filth that had been eating at me for so long.

Eventually I graduated from the initial treatment and entered an aftercare program provided by Fairview Southdale Hospital.[4] I began to attend a Vietnam veterans' rap group meeting at the Vet Center in St. Paul and later began meeting regularly with a read-

---

4   Champus (now Tri-Care), a program for military or retired military personnel in civilian life, paid for my alcoholism treatment.

justment counselor named Ernie Boswell. As a clinical psychologist, Dr. Boswell would play a major role in helping me clear a remaining hurdle in my life—my explosive anger. I also continued attending AA, which I had joined during treatment.

MAKING PEACE WITH FAMILY

Looking back, I consider all of 1988 and first few months of 1989 as a time in my life when I made a major course correction and saw broken relationships mended. I stayed sober and clean and made friends with many other recovering addicts. My relationship with my daughter Pam was also improving. We'd go out to a local coffee shop and talk until the wee hours of the morning.

My decision to take responsibility for my life also helped heal my relationship with my parents, then in their upper 70s. Proudly, I drove my specially-equipped van downtown and took my dad for several rides. Due to her physical limitations, Mom had a hard time getting up into the van, but I even took her for a ride one day by lowering the lift.

At length, I asked my mom and dad to forgive me for all the trouble I had caused. I assured them that they had done a good job of raising me, taking me to Sunday school, and trying to get me into the church. "The problems I had were not your fault," I stated, as I told them of my happiness at finally being sober. They spoke of their happiness, too, with my decisions to stop drinking and smoking dope and to get treatment. "He's going to be okay now," my dad told another man one day.

Now, I wanted to feel everything, express everything, and enjoy everything. I'm sure I came off to some people as a zealous ex-drunk, but I didn't care. For years I had tried to avoid my feelings by drinking them into the ground. Besides smothering the pain, I had suppressed any real joy, and I'm not sure I even knew what love was. Getting off the drugs and alcohol, I had to start dealing with my feelings.

Some of my feelings were bad—like how I had treated women in my life. I'd used them for sex and to buy me alcohol if they were older than me. I didn't care about them; all I cared about was me and getting high. But some feelings were good—like my affection for family and friends. I began to take great delight in verbalizing my love for them and in expressing my gratitude for all who stuck by me over the years.

The other change I can identify at that time in my life is that I began giving credit for the good things happening to me—my sobriety, my growing independence, my healed relationships, and my newfound feelings—to Jesus Christ. He either pushed me directly or indirectly to make these changes. I knew then, for sure, that he was working in my life and that I was a believer. I began to realize that he had always been literally inches from me—saving me in the rocket attack, helping me as I struggled to survive the trip home, and sustaining me during a lengthy physical rehabilitation.

Today, I can look back at the late 1980s and see his hands everywhere in my life, sometimes prodding me directly and at other times encouraging me through other people he had placed alongside me.

After joining AA, I developed a routine of reading a devotional thought each morning and then talking with my Savior, often in the manner of a friend chatting with a friend. "Good morning, Lord!" I began. "Thank you for this beautiful sunshine." I was developing a real relationship with the Lord Jesus Christ. My habit of conversing with the Savior, informal at times and more formal at others, continues to this day.

I had come a long way, but I still had important things to learn.

CHAPTER 15

Taking Responsibility

HENNEPIN COUNTY MEDICAL CENTER
MINNEAPOLIS, MINNESOTA

FALL 1990

Mother lay motionless in the hospital bed, her breathing assisted by a respirator.

My dad had died the year before. He had developed lung cancer and was being treated for a large tumor protruding into his esophagus. He went into cardiac arrest and lost blood pressure. They just couldn't revive him.

Mother took Dad's death very hard. She had always depended on him, and living alone in the four-plex they had owned since 1950 was difficult. Then one day in the fall of 1990, I got a call that my mother had suffered a heart attack and paramedics had taken her to the Hennepin County Medical Center. When I drove downtown to see her, she was awake and talking. But the heart attack had done a great deal of damage, and Mother got progressively weaker.

I remember one of my visits to her hospital room. I had positioned my wheelchair next to the head of her bed.

"Mother, the Lord is with us," I told her.

"Where is Jesus?" she asked.

"He's here with us," I said.

"I can't see him, but I can see his shoes," she replied with a hint of delirium—or perhaps she really did.

Another time when she had not responded for hours, I sang to her a childhood song, "Jesus loves me this I know, for the Bible tells me so." Without opening her eyes, she replied, "Yes, I know that Jesus loves me." Her lucid periods became less and less frequent, however. Eventually the hospital staff put her on a respirator and inserted a feeding tube.

As Mother's condition worsened, her personal physician and the nursing staff began talking with me about removing the respirator and letting her go. "She's brain-dead, and there is no possibility of her coming back," they argued. I resisted. My brother LeRoy had died in 1987, and I had lost my dad the previous year. I was not ready to let my mother go, and my daughter Pam had grown very close to her in recent years. Besides, as head of the family, I desperately wanted to take responsibility and make the right decision by applying my rediscovered faith. In this real-life situation, I was uncertain if God's Word, which speaks passionately of respect for human life, would allow us to remove a device keeping Mother alive.

Our family met with our pastor, DeLloyd Wippich of Trinity First Lutheran Church. This meeting included Mother's doctor, her nurses, Mother's cardiologist, a neurologist, and a medical ethicist.

The neurologist, who had been brought in to consult on her condition, disputed the idea that she was brain-dead. "There is still brain activity," she stated. More support came for keeping her on the respirator when her cardiologist, Dr. Fine, said he believed Mother could recover. "She will probably never be well enough to return home, but perhaps to a nursing facility." Encouraged by these comments, we made the decision to stay the course.

However as Mother's condition continued to deteriorate, I appreciated Pastor Wippich's council. He assured us that it would be okay to remove the respirator, but he advised us against removing the feeding tube. "The church's view is that the respirator is artificial life-support," he reasoned, "but everyone needs food to live." His words assured us that whatever decision we made, God would not look at us as murderers. Until then, I had resisted removing the respirator, but I agreed to it with the acceptance of the rest of the family.

To our delight, after the hospital staff took the respirator off, Mother lived several months and then something even more amazing happened. She woke up from her coma. We had moved her to a nursing home on Nicollet Avenue in Bloomington to make it easier for family and friends to visit. One day my daughter Pam, who lived across from the nursing home, came over to see her and immediately called me. "I have news that will knock you out of your wheelchair," she said. "Grandma is awake and coherent." My mother couldn't talk, but she could gesture, and she knew who Pam was. She was wide awake, after medical personal had told us she was brain-dead. What a comeback!

Mother stayed awake and alert for a couple of weeks. Then she became ill with a common virus that infected many of the residents and even the staff of the nursing home, and her system was too weak to handle it. She lapsed into a coma, and within a few days, she was gone.

I handled all this fairly well because of my faith. Without my faith, I would have had a much harder time losing most of my immediate family in a short period of time. The only one left was my sister Carol, who was totally deaf and who, in her early 20s had been diagnosed with paranoid schizophrenia. Carol now lived in a group home in Minneapolis. As her closest relative, I assumed responsibility for her. Making sure Carol had what she needed and settling my family's finances preoccupied me for quite a while. Mother had put my name on her bank account but the four-plex remained in my parents' names, so the estate had to be settled before I could liquidate the property and use the money to take care of Carol.

MORE BAD DECISIONS

Not much happened in the months and years following my mother's death. Day after day, I'd visit the local Byerly's supermarket to drink coffee and smoke cigarettes with friends. Although I had plenty of friends to hang out with, I wasn't dating anyone. Then, in 1996, I became romantically involved with a woman named Linda who I had met about seven years earlier at an AA meeting.

We started dating in late summer of '96, and she moved into my Bloomington home soon afterward. She wanted to get married right away, but I talked her into waiting until September of the following year.

I admit suspecting, during our engagement, that this marriage would not work. For one thing, Linda took a trip with her sister to Florida. While there, she called to tell me of her decision to start drinking again. "It's just a glass of wine at dinner," she reasoned, but for a recovering alcoholic, that one glass can be a ticket back into the depths of the disease. Then there was Linda's family, who had accepted me with open arms. They also liked to drink and frequently invited us over to parties. Linda would drink with them, while I wanted to leave. I knew better than to hang with people using alcohol; I had moved into this relationship too quickly.

Despite these early indicators, I did not break my engagement with Linda. For one thing, I had told everyone that we were getting married, and although I was still a novice at this, I was trying to live my faith. In the Bible, I read about Joseph's engagement to Mary and how he considered breaking it after learning Mary was pregnant by the Holy Spirit; but he didn't. Joseph's commitment impressed me, so I figured that I needed heavy duty reasons for breaking my engagement to Linda.

To be very honest, I had already made one bad choice. Linda and I were sexually involved before marriage, which was not morally or biblically right. Since we were already in bed together, I had convinced myself that the right thing to do would be to marry Linda. Actually, I was about to make yet another bad choice.

We did get married in September and honeymooned in Las Vegas. I recall feeling tired one evening and just wanting to go up to our hotel room and go to sleep, but Linda wanted to stay up. So after helping me settle in, she went back down to the casino. She burned through a lot of money and booze that night, returning to our room around 4:00 a.m.

At that point, right after our wedding, I realized her drinking and gambling was getting progressively worse. Our first year of marriage bore that out. She spent a lot of time at casinos, and her abuse of alcohol increased. Moreover, her attitude toward spiritual things began to change. Before marriage, we talked a lot about my desire to live my faith, and she had been supportive. Now when I asked her to church, she'd say, "Sure, I'll go with you." But often she'd be out at a casino and late to the worship service.

To top it off, we fought a lot. Both Linda and I had anger issues.

So like the hypocrite I was, I threw a big birthday party for Linda a little more than one year after our wedding, and soon afterwards I told her I was divorcing her.

Isn't there anyone for me . . .

You wouldn't think that a triple amputee would have so many problems with women. The trouble was, I was unsure of the women in my life and unsure of myself. I seemed to move ahead in my relationships too quickly, perhaps thinking that they'd be gone if I didn't. Such was the case with Ruth, who was my aide when I decided to divorce Linda. As my marriage to Linda deteriorated, I grew close to Ruth and, although we didn't have sex before the divorce, we were definitely emotionally involved.

When I announced I was divorcing Linda, Ruth quit as my aide. It looked better that way. Then, when the divorce was final in December 1997, she came back and soon we were sexually involved. But it didn't last long. Although Ruth proclaimed her Christianity, she and I differed on many issues concerning faith. On top of that, I still had very bad anger issues and could blow up without warning. It affected my relationship with Ruth to the point where her father, who practiced psychology in Missouri, advised her that I might have serious mental health problems. We broke up February of 1998.

"Isn't there a woman out there for me?" I thought, remorseful at the way I had handled my dealings with females. At age fifty-four, I was beginning to wonder, as were many of my soldier friends. A majority of us had problems with communication, rage, and divorce—symptoms of PTSD. Talking with them and recounting my own poor track record planted an idea in my mind that would grow to maturity in a very short time. I must find a way to put brakes on my anger if I ever expect to succeed at marriage.

My next try at marriage came sooner than expected. That same spring, I looked through the "personals" in the classified section of the *Minneapolis Star Tribune* and came upon this ad: "Single, divorced female looking for single white male . . . someone to walk, bike, and go to dinner and movies with." The ad ended with a Scripture reference (2 Corinthians 6:14[1]) and a telephone number.

I showed the classified to my aide, Rondi, who was preparing my supper. "Why not call her right now," suggested Rondi.

"I've got to think about it," I replied, still smarting from my recent failures.

"You're not going to get anything to eat until you call her," declared Rondi, so I retreated into my bedroom and picked up the phone.

I was nervous about calling because, as I assumed from the presence of a scripture reference in her ad, she must be a good Christian woman. I had, on the other hand, proven to be a less-than-good Christian man. Fortunately, I got this woman's answering machine so I didn't have to stutter or stammer. I simply mentioned seeing her ad and said I was interested in talking with her. I left my phone number, thanked her, and hung up.

A day or two went by and I finally got a call from Eydie, the woman who had placed the ad. We talked for a while, and before

---

1   2 Corinthians 6:14: "Do not be yoked together with unbelievers. For what do righteousness and wickedness have in common?" (NIV)

we said goodbye I told her of my disability. "I'm a triple amputee," I explained. "Both arms are gone, one leg is gone, and the other is pretty useless, but I have artificial arms, drive a van, and am fairly independent." I do not remember anything else I told her. I was very nervous.

We talked a couple more times by phone and then decided to meet for coffee at Byerly's in Edina. As I looked for a parking spot, I saw a woman wearing sunglasses who matched Eydie's self-description. She smiled, and I parked and rolled over to introduce myself. We went inside and got some coffee. "I'll pay if you'll carry the coffee," I quipped. We had a good hour-and-a-half visit, which included talking about our religious beliefs.

When I got home, my other aide Lori asked me, "So what do you think?" I said, "Well, I think Eydie and I will become good friends, but I think that's as far as it will go." I added, "This is a classy woman, and I'm not in her class." Besides, she said in her ad that she wanted someone to walk and bike with.

I was wrong again—so what's new? Over the next couple of months Eydie and I talked several times by phone and met in such memorable locations as the now-extinct Borders bookstore in Plymouth, Chili's restaurant along south Highway 100, and finally at my home in Bloomington. Rondi cooked a steak dinner for us, and we sat out on the patio for hours, sipping coffee and talking.

After that date, Eydie started coming down to Bloomington every weekend from her home in Plymouth and her job as administrative assistant at Quality Assured Label in Hopkins. We began to get serious about our relationship to the point where, in July 1998, we circled the topic of marriage by discussing subjects like adult children, finances, and even the possibility of meeting with Eydie's pastor.

One event underlined both the difficulty ahead for Eydie and her tenacity. We took a walk in my neighborhood on a day that looked like rain. "I don't know if we should," she hesitated. I looked up and saw the sun peaking through the clouds and said, "I don't think it will rain—let's go." So we walked quite a ways from the house and ended up on Old Shakopee Road, almost in front of my church. All of a sudden, the sky opened and we were caught in a downpour.

Eydie and her dog Natasha made it to the church first. I followed in my electric wheelchair at full speed when BANG! the controls failed, and I came to an abrupt halt. "I'm dead in the water," I yelled to Eydie, as I tried to put the chair into manual mode. "You're going to have to push me."

So back into the rain dove Eydie. I'll let her tell the story from here:

> **Eydie**: *"By the time I got Ron up under the overhang of the church, we were totally soaked. Finally, the rain let up. I hooked Natasha to the wheelchair and pushed Ron all the way home. Ron immediately called one of his aides, Amanda, and asked her to come over to help him. In his panic, he totally ignored me—it was all about him. Amanda walked in with a hair dryer and began*

drying him off, while I stood there dripping wet. At that
point I just went home. It was a real learning experience
for me as to what I would face in marrying a man with
a disability."

Despite my lack of chivalry, Eydie and I continued to date, and
in September we got engaged. Eydie proposed a December wedding, but with my previous track record, I held out for a longer engagement. We compromised on February 7, 1999 and held a small
wedding in our Bloomington home.

Since this was Eydie's second time at the altar and my third, we
both wanted this marriage to work. As a Christian, Eydie prayed
that the Lord would warn her if she was falling in love with the
wrong man. "I looked for the red flags," she states, "but they never
appeared." Coming from a less mature spiritual position, I still had
a lot of anger and confusion inside. I was afraid of divorce and of
losing another wife—of being hoodwinked and taken for a ride—
as I had with Anne and Linda. In the end, I decided to roll the dice
one more time.

We had a nice wedding, with some of our friends and relatives
in attendance. Both of my daughters attended, even though they
had had reservations about our relationship at the beginning. Everyone, including the bride and the groom, seemed happy.

But that happiness would soon be severely tested by a series of
emotional eruptions that threatened this latest sacred commitment.

CHAPTER 16

Brakes on My Anger

STRATEGIC AIR & SPACE MUSEUM
ASHLAND, NEBRASKA

JULY 2000

Both Eydie and I possess strong wills. We had had a few fights while dating and during our brief engagement. In these bouts my anger quickly escalated and just as quickly dissipated, leaving Eydie bewildered and without a clue that she had witnessed a recurring problem.

I knew my tendency to get extremely angry without warning and that I usually handled the situation poorly. Perhaps that is why I dragged my feet at setting a wedding date. I had a desire for a physical relationship with a woman, but I didn't want to go against God's will again by engaging in it outside of marriage. On the other hand, I just didn't think I'd be able to maintain the relationship, and I definitely did not want to go through another divorce.

After our engagement, the frequency of my angry outbursts increased. I'll let Eydie describe one of these seismic events.

> **Eydie:** *"I was at Ron's house in Bloomington when his daughter Rhonda dropped by. Ron and Rhonda got into a discussion which quickly turned into an argument. Though I did not take Rhonda's side, I indicated that I understood what she was saying. That was the end of it, or so I thought.*
>
> *"Before Rhonda arrived, Ron and I had made plans to drive to the nearby suburb of Edina. When she left, we got into his van and started out. Soon we began talking about his disagreement with Rhonda, and the intensity of our conversation rapidly escalated. All of a sudden, Ron's anger went over the top. He accused me of taking Rhonda's side. I tried to defend myself, but he wouldn't listen and began using horrible language that I had never before heard from him. He verbally abused me and obviously took pleasure in my pain. I began to cry and told Ron to pull into a nearby parking lot. 'I'm done with this argument,' I said and got out of the van.*
>
> *"As quickly as it flared, Ron's temper de-escalated—a pattern I would witness many times in the months ahead. I agreed to get back in the van, and we talked about what had just happened. It never crossed my mind that he had*

anger issues which could eventually jeopardize our mar-
riage. I thought he'd just gotten mad at me and blew up."

Both Eydie and I would later describe our life together as good, except for my occasional but persistent eruptions of rage. During our first year of marriage, we began meeting as a couple with Dr. Ernie Boswell, the psychologist who led my Vietnam Vets rap group. We asked Dr. Boswell to help us figure out what caused me to explode without warning.

During this time, we worked on getting to know each other better so as to avoid misunderstandings. Dr. Boswell also counseled us to avoid what he called "stuffing the musket." Instead of dealing with little irritations when they happened, I'd stuff my emotions inside me until I had built up a huge barrel of anger. Then "KA-BOOM." I'd unload on the people closest to me—usually my wife. Here are some of her recollections:

> **Eydie:** *"Each time Ron's anger exploded, it followed a similar pattern. He would bring up issues from months before, and I'd say, 'If you were angry at me for something I was doing back then, why didn't you just stop and tell me?' But he didn't know how to do that, so when the musket was full, he'd unload it on me.*
>
> *"At the peak of his rage, he'd use obscenities as tools to hurt me. He knew just what I'd do if he said the 'f' word—I'd turn my back, walk into the bedroom, and shut the door. Then he'd say, 'come on out' and I'd say,*

'no, we're done talking tonight.' Then he'd angrily repeat phrases like, 'I'm worthless, I'm an awful husband, and I'm not good enough for you.' He'd add, 'You should just leave me and get a divorce lawyer.' He'd offer to support me while I'd get an apartment, and I'd tell him, 'I came into this marriage with nothing and I can very well walk out without anything.' But I didn't want to do that. I loved Ron and wanted to make it work."

We had begun counseling with Dr. Boswell prior to our Colorado trip, and he'd suggested exercises like "Communicating within the Model" where we'd sit across the table from each other and I'd say, "I'm angry with you." Eydie would say, "You're angry with me?" And I'd say, "Yes, I'm angry because . . ." and then I'd name the thing that disturbed me. The goal was to explain why I was angry, to avoid stuffing my musket. It also helped Eydie to stop and listen to what I was saying, because she would have to repeat what I said word for word. That way, I knew she was listening to me. Likewise, I would have to repeat everything Eydie said, which made me listen more closely to her side of the story.

The exercise helped a little, but we still had not come to a point where my unpredictable explosions of anger had been significantly reduced by the time we embarked on our delayed honeymoon in July 2000.

Eydie's family had planned a Colorado reunion the year after our wedding, so we decided to make that road trip our official honeymoon. During that road trip the trouble brewing in our young relationship came to a head—a nuclear warhead that produced an ominous mushroom cloud over our fledgling marriage.

The time in Colorado with family had gone well. Then on the way back to Minnesota from the reunion, we stopped at the Strategic Air & Space Museum at Ashland, Nebraska. Eydie can explain in greater detail what happened that day. Frankly, I can't remember much of it, but I know it was bad.

> **Eydie:** *"We stopped at the museum and went in together. I had my camera along, and I told Ron that I was going to take some pictures. For the next hour, I walked all over the building taking pictures. I assumed Ron would wander around while I was gone and look at whatever he wanted to, then we'd look through the museum together.*

> *"But when I returned, I found Ron in the same place where I'd left him, and he was extremely upset with me. He told me later that he thought I had left him to look at the museum alone. However, when he begins to explode, like he did in the lobby of the museum that July afternoon, he'll often point to something he's angry about— but that's not the real reason.*

> *"Trying to smooth over the situation, I said, 'Come on, Ron, let's go into the museum. We haven't seen it together yet.' To which he replied, 'I don't care. I'm done. We're going home!' From then on everything he said was over the top. He used the same hurtful language and patronizing phrases I've described earlier.*

"Eventually, we got back in the van and drove back to Minneapolis without saying another word to each other."

RETHINKING THE NUCLEAR OPTION

The day after we arrived home, Eydie made an appointment to see Dr. Boswell alone. As the psychologist seated her in his office, he asked a probing question, "Are you ready to quit yet?" Now, Eydie will tell you that Dr. Boswell had treated her very fairly in our counseling sessions, despite the fact that he and I had been friends for years and that she was my third wife, but I don't think he really expected her to stay. He was mistaken.

"I am not going to quit," said Eydie firmly. After describing my explosion of anger at the air and space museum, she declared. "I want something that will make this better."

"There is an anti-psychotic drug called risperidone," said Dr. Boswell. "It could have some serious side effects, but it might help." He explained to Eydie that risperidone works on a human being the way a governor works on a car. It slows the rate at which a person's anger rises, giving him or her time to become self-aware and assess the cost of escalating the fight.

Before our Colorado trip, I had decided not to go back to Dr. Boswell. The anger management techniques we'd been trying didn't seem to help my outbursts that much. But when Eydie came home with news of a drug I could take, I jumped at it—even after she explained the downside. Dr. Boswell had warned her that a small number of people taking this drug develop serious side effects that are not reversible. These people may be seen in nursing homes, with their heads hanging down and dragging their feet.[1]

"I don't care about the risks," I told Eydie, "If there is a chance it will help me with my anger, I'll try it." That same day, I made an appointment to see Dr. Boswell, who in turn asked psychiatrist Dr. Suck Won Kim to prescribe my risperidone treatment. He also gave me a book called *Emotional Intelligence* by Daniel Goleman, which helped me to better understand myself, to become more aware of my growing anger, and to stop and ask, "Is this debate or argument really worth a nuclear explosion?"

As a kid, I'd get so angry when I didn't get my way that I'd shout, "I don't care what happens—I hope it kills me!" I remember my mother telling me that I had self-destructive characteristics. "At least you don't want to hurt others," she said. "It's you who you want to destroy." That's not quite right, because in the middle of my rage I would intentionally hurt people with my words, but that memory tells me my anger issues go way back to childhood. My anger was not something that happened solely because of PTSD, Vietnam, or my alcohol abuse, although those factors may have exacerbated the problem.

Dr. Boswell labeled the process of anger escalation leading to my explosions of rage as "catastrophic thinking." I'd conclude that the world was coming to an end over a little thing like my wheel-

---

1   Known as tardive dyskinesia, this condition can result from taking certain antipsychotic drugs over a long period of time.

chair breaking down, leaving me unable to move. Blinded by my immediate frustration, I'd become unreasonable. Seeing no hope for the future, I'd be willing to vent my rage and destroy the relationships around me.

In short, the risperidone slowed down that process, giving me time to weigh the value of acting out my anger against the potential hurtful results. It gave me an opportunity to pause and calm down, since I had not yet crossed the line of losing control.

> **Eydie:** *"Risperidone was an incredible tool. After Ron began taking the medication, he had only one or two more explosive outbursts, and then they were gone."*

When I began taking risperidone, Dr. Kim worked with me to monitor and adjust the medication. I was still attending a rap group for veterans, and during those sessions I could see Dr. Boswell watching me closely for any harmful effects of the drug. Thankfully none ever presented themselves, although Dr. Kim later took me off the drug because he thought it might be causing me to gain too much weight.

As for our relationship today, Eydie and I rarely fight, which is a miracle for two such strong-willed people. But I've since learned that she is not out to hurt or destroy me. (You see, I had based much of my anger on my fears: in particular the fear of being taken advantage of and the fear of desertion—perhaps related to being left for dead in Vietnam.) Instead, I've come to trust and love Eydie more as the years have progressed.

At times, I still become angry with Eydie, and she gets angry with me. That is a normal part of being a married couple. But with the help of the medication and a greater awareness of what is going on inside, I've learned better ways to deal with my anger.

Travel opens new vistas

Something that has unlocked a whole new world for me is the ability to travel. This began when Eydie thought it might be nice for us to go on a cruise. I scoffed at her idea, declaring, "With my disability, that's totally impossible!" I could drive and had taken some trips—even stayed in hotels, but I had the idea from my time in the military that all ships had small compartments, and I just couldn't conceive of being able to maneuver my wheelchair in that space. Plus, we would have to fly to go on a cruise, and I didn't see how that could work either.

With Eydie's persistent prodding, however, we contacted an Owatonna, Minnesota agency called Flying Wheels Travel. There we met a woman named Christine Demming who changed our outlook on travel for the physically disabled and gave me hope that I could go places I never thought possible. One of the first things she did was to arrange for a friend who worked for Sun Country Airlines to take me aboard a plane and show me how they could accommodate my disability. Chris then proceeded to dispel my misconceptions of cruise ship accessibility.

Since then, we've taken two Caribbean cruises and an Alaskan cruise. We've also traveled to Washington, DC, Disney World, the

Black Hills, Las Vegas, Nashville, and San Francisco. All this began by Eydie saying, "Let's just look into it and see what things are possible." In fact, there have been times recently when Eydie thinks something's impossible and I say, "No, it can be done."

That's amazing when you consider my hopeless outlook and my total dependence on others in the decade after returning from Vietnam. But turn the page, and I'll tell you something EVEN MORE AMAZING.

CHAPTER 17

Real Healing

Bloomington, Minnesota

Fall 2012

My many wounds (both external and internal) did not have a single origin and were not inflicted all at once. Most of my physical wounds originated with the 3:10 a.m. rocket attack in Vietnam, but my predilection to self-inflicted wounds—like my explosive temper and my alcoholism—may have had genetic roots. My mother had a violent temper and members of my immediate and extended family had a history of mental instability.[1] However, wrong choices I made early in life clearly deepened and prevented the healing of those wounds. In the process of making those choices, I wounded

---

1 It should be noted that the VA Hospital medical staff has insisted over the years that I am perfectly sane.

the people closest to me—my parents, my first wife Judie, and my daughters Pam and Rhonda.

Nor did the healing of these many wounds come through the administration of one medical marvel, but from a number of sources including countless surgeries, pharmaceuticals, relationship-building tools, caregivers, pastors, family, and friends which Providence supplied at just the right time to bring about my present contentment as a sixty-eight-year-old retired U.S. Air Force sergeant and American citizen.

My physical healing from the rocket attack took months and years as surgeons worked to salvage as much mobility as possible and give me the opportunity to be as active as I wanted to be. However, it took more than a decade and a divorce before I began to experience the health and wholeness of independence. It was nearly another decade before I accepted responsibility for my addiction, and still another decade until I learned to manage my rage.

I would be remiss if I did not reveal to you, the reader, my source of real healing. There is a unifying theme in my life that has grown stronger as I've aged and to which I attribute the healing of all the wounds described in this book. As a small boy, I had heard of and believed in a God who loved me and sent his son Jesus Christ to die on a cross in payment for my sins. As I grew to manhood, I believed in the existence of this God but refused opportunities to know him or to follow his way. Instead, I made up my own rules for life. When hot shrapnel fell around me as I lay on the ground at

Da Nang Air Base in 1967, my rules proved useless. In desperation, I called out to God.

The medical teams in Vietnam, Guam, and Texas patched me up physically and sent me back to Minnesota. Unprepared to face the future—and uninformed of the ways of the God to whom I had called in my distress—I defaulted again to my own rules. Yet, I knew there must be more. So I began reading the Bible. My desire to read, understand, and apply God's Word to my life continued and increased even as my dependency, my alcoholism, and my anger tore apart my most intimate relationships.

Finally, I hit bottom and entered treatment for my addictions. I was a broken man.

Some choose not to believe in God as they go through treatment or attend AA meetings. They identify their higher power as an unknown force, a tree, or the group of people they're meeting with. As for me, my higher power is the God of the Bible. Without him and without the forgiveness, grace, and hope he offers, I would be dead by now. My death may have come from the rocket blast, or from alcohol, or by my own hand, because I could never ever have accepted myself if I had remained the way I was.

Having the understanding I do today of God's Word and having lived on this earth for almost seven decades, I can confidently state that my primary trouble in this life was not what happened to me on an air base in Vietnam, but the evil and selfishness inside me. Although intensified by PTSD, my alcoholism and my rage stemmed from my desire to have my own way—to make my own rules.

But in God's great mercy, he heard me. He did not abandon me. He reached down and rescued me from both physical and spiritual death. Without him, I could not have made it either on the battlefield of Vietnam or on the fighting plains of life. Since then, I have received his wonderful liberation from human dependency, from alcoholism, and from rage.

In this last great battle, God gave me the tools—through Dr. Boswell, through the prescription of risperidone, through a new awareness of myself, and through a growing dependence on him—to deal with my anger. Now, as I read God's Word daily, the reality of the Bible stories taught to me as a child have come to life. It all makes sense. Everything else in the theater of life—politics, status, my own selfish desires, and so on—fades into the background. What has taken center stage is my desire to get closer to God and to know him better. I now love my Creator and love those around me because he first loved and rescued me.

Knowing this God, in whom I have believed in all my life but in whom I've really just begun to trust, has given me tremendous peace.

My wife Eydie and I have a wonderful marriage. I have a good relationship with my two daughters and their families. I've reunited with my friend Cliff Thielman *(see Chapters 4-8)* who served with me in Duluth and then Vietnam and who, at one point in the 1970s, refused to take my drunken phone calls. I've had the opportunity to reconnect with one of my nurses, Elaine Carlson, and my surgeon, Dr. Michael Gurvey, both of whom cared for me in 1967 at Wilford Hall. Most recently, my first wife Judie accepted an invitation to come over to our house. I apologized to her for all the terrible things I had said and the misery and pain I put her through for thirteen years following my return from Vietnam. I asked her forgiveness for my unfaithfulness even before that. We had a good talk and parted as friends.

Most importantly, I have the hope of eternal life. I know Jesus Christ has saved me from my sin, and all the trash, garbage, vomit, and filth of my past life is gone. God, my heavenly father, sees me through the eyes of his son Jesus, as perfect, clean and righteous. When I die, he will accept me into his presence with great joy. That's REAL healing.

---

*"For you, Lord, have delivered my soul from death, my
eyes from tears, my feet from stumbling, that I may walk
before the Lord in the land of the living."*
–Psalm 116:8-9 (NIV)

You may contact Ron Schwerman at:
www.brokenbutnotabandoned.com

APPENDIX 1

Help for PTSD- Afflicted Vets

P TSD (Post-traumatic Stress Disorder) is a mental health condition brought on by a horrific event witnessed or personally experienced. That makes veterans of military campaigns particularly susceptible to PTSD. A soldier suffering PTSD need not have been assigned a combat role but may (as in my case) be injured or otherwise traumatized while working in a support role within a combat or disaster zone.

According to the National Center for PTSD at the U.S. Department of Veterans Affairs, symptoms of PTSD include reliving the event through flashbacks in your waking moments or in your dreams, avoiding situations that remind you of the event, feeling numb or feeling keyed up.[1]

---

1   "What is PTSD?," United States Department of Veterans Affairs: National Center for PTSD (United States Department of Veterans Affairs), http://www.ptsd.va.gov/public/pages/what-is-ptsd.asp. (accessed August 30, 2012.)

Problems like hopelessness, depression, drinking and drugs, physical symptoms or chronic pain, employment troubles, and relationship dysfunction (such as divorce) may be brought on or amplified by PTSD.[2]

I experienced upsetting dreams (night sweats), emotional numbness and angry outbursts, hopelessness and depression, problems in my relationships, and self-destructive behavior like alcohol abuse and suicidal thoughts. Other PTSD sufferers avoid talking or even thinking about the trauma, avoid activities once enjoyed, experience memory problems and trouble concentrating, are easily startled, or hear and see things that aren't there.[3]

Counseling and medication have both been proven effective in treating PTSD.

A veteran's first line of defense

The best opportunity for early PTSD intervention exists immediately upon the veteran's return home, says Dr. Ernest Boswell, a clinical psychologist with an emphasis on PTSD diagnosis and treatment. "One of the most disabling things a family can do is to sign onto a conspiracy of silence," states Dr. Boswell. "The veteran will not acknowledge that they've changed and the family senses they have changed, but they don't want to rock the boat."

---

2   "What is PTSD?"

3   Mayo Clinic Staff, "Post-traumatic Stress Disorder (PTSD)," MayoClinic, http://www.mayclinic.com/health/post-traumatic-stress-disorder/DS00246 (accessed August 30, 2012)

Families often take the attitude that they don't want to confront changes in their veterans but instead give them time to decompress. "That decompression time just allows them to go more and more out of control," says Boswell, himself a veteran of the Vietnam War. "By the time the [PTSD] gets to a critical point, in some cases there is not much else we can do."

In 2008, Dr. Boswell served as a consultant to the Minnesota National Guard's Yellow Ribbon Team which devised the guard's re-integration training. Previously, guard members returning from combat were allowed generous personal liberty with no requirement for assembly or drill activity. "What often happened was that the [veteran] would disengage from the family, get together with the people they served with, and go out drinking," states Boswell. "The whole thing would spiral from there." So Minnesota's National Guard decided against decompression time and in favor of engaging returning soldiers in re-integration events.

However, the first line of defense against PTSD is the soldier's family, contends Dr. Boswell, who has over thirty years of clinical experience. "The family needs to be the agent that compassionately holds their loved one's feet to the fire," he states. "If you are the veteran's father or spouse, you need to say to them, 'Something is not the same. I'm not blaming you, but I'm not going to sit here and pretend it doesn't exist. Either we have to talk about it or you have to get in and talk to someone about it.'"

Dr. Boswell notes that veterans are more likely to seek services when family members agree to stand with the veteran. The conversation might play out like this: "You have a problem that is affecting all of us. I have your back, and we will do this together, but you're the one with the services—you have to ask for the help."

For services available to veterans and their families, visit the National Center for PTSD at http://www.ptsd.va.gov/index.asp.

APPENDIX 2

A Spouse's Perspective

I've been asked what advice I would give spouses of veterans with disabilities, looking back over my nearly fourteen years of marriage to Ron. My first thought is that I am the last person to give marriage advice. God knows I have made serious mistakes in my life and former marriage.

I was not aware that Ron had anger issues when we got married. In reality, there were two issues on which I probably should have sought counsel before we got married. First, I was contemplating marriage to a veteran of the Vietnam War—a terrible conflict which produced long-lasting effects (including PTSD) in the lives of most veterans who participated. Second, I was marrying a man who was severely disabled. One of these factors alone should have given me pause. I literally prayed that God would send up a red flag if there was any reason I should not marry Ron. At the time, I didn't see any red flags.

I believe that God blesses believers and unbelievers alike. If you are not a follower of Christ, you can still have a happy marriage, but I am here to tell you that Ron and I would never have made it without a God-honoring life and marriage. He is and has been our rock—our firm foundation.

To other spouses and veterans: remember the person you fell in love with at the very beginning. What are the qualities that attracted you in the first place? That person is still there. Experiences like war do change people—they add baggage to any marriage. You have to remember that Satan HATES marriage.[1] He does his best to destroy it, but with your determination and God's help, YOU CAN OVERCOME. I strongly believe that without Christ in our lives and marriages, it is too easy to quit. Ron's and my marriage would not have had a chance without our strong faith in God.

Satan will tell you:

- That you deserve to be happy
- That you didn't bargain for this
- That you don't know this person anymore
- That he'd be better off without you
- That she deserves better than you
- That you don't have to put up with this anymore
- . . . and more lies

The truth is, God has joined you both in marriage, and you are now one. What are you willing to do to save your marriage and make it work? You must approach marriage determined not to quit.

---

1 Satan hates a good marriage because it typifies the relationship Jesus Christ has promised to his bride, the church.

My advice to husbands and wives of veterans who are struggling or have lost what they once had is simply this: help is available. There is more help for husbands and wives of veterans now than there ever was for many years after Vietnam. But you must ask for it. You cannot do this alone. When help is offered:

- Find a counselor who is experienced with veterans and PTSD
- Be willing to listen honestly to advice
- Be willing to work together—it definitely takes both of you
- Do not expect instant answers
- Be patient with yourself and your spouse
- Be willing to work—marriage is a full-time job
- Be willing to change

It will not be easy being married to a disabled veteran. He or she absolutely has special needs and expectations. I cannot speak to husbands of veterans, but to the wives I say that I believe we are uniquely gifted as caregivers. After all, we have been gifted by God to be mothers—the highest calling of a caregiver. This does not mean, however, that we are to "mother" our husbands. But we can empower them, as the U.S. Army declares, "To be all they can be."

Above all:

- Be an encourager
- Be affirming
- Be his/her greatest fan

- Be proud of him/her
- Be his/her lover and best friend

Most importantly, COMMUNICATE, COMMUNICATE, COMMUNICATE. This is something you have heard many times, but it is still one of the most necessary ingredients in a marriage. It sounds easy but is very difficult. It may even take practice.

I have given lots of advice here. But I want to make it clear that I am not a perfect spouse to my disabled veteran by any stretch of the imagination. These are mostly lessons that God has taught me, and I am continuing to learn and grow through my second marriage. I am selfish, stubborn, and impatient to a fault. But I was willing to change and determined to make my marriage work. You can do it, too.

God will be your coach, and I will be your cheerleader. The rewards will last for the rest of your lives together. Keep focused; it is not about what you can do or what your veteran can do. It is about what GOD can do working through both of you. He gets the glory—you get a happy, healthy marriage!

Blessings,
Eydie Schwerman

You may contact Eydie at:
www.brokenbutnotabandoned.com